AF261449

SYMBOLISM

Author: Alfred Hunt

Layout:
Baseline Co. Ltd,
District 3, Ho Chi Minh City
Vietnam

ISBN: 978-1-68325-939-8

Printed in

Alfred Hunt

SYMBOLISM

Myth, allegory, and visions of the unseen

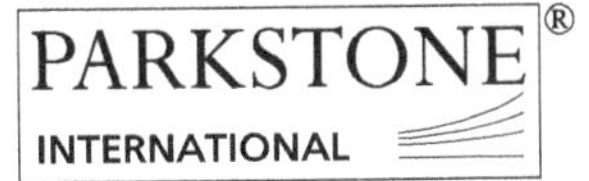

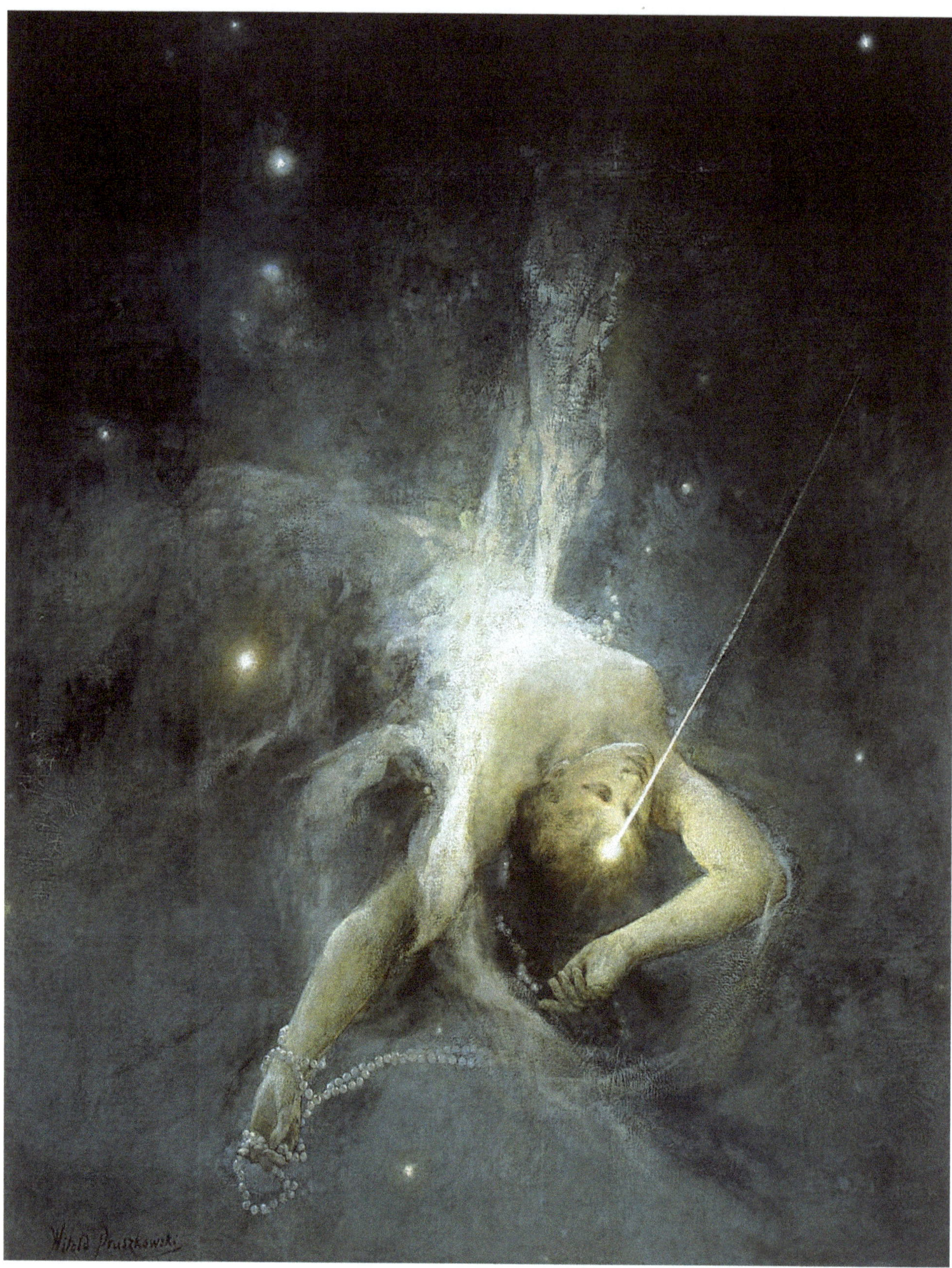

Witold Pruszkowski

CONTENTS

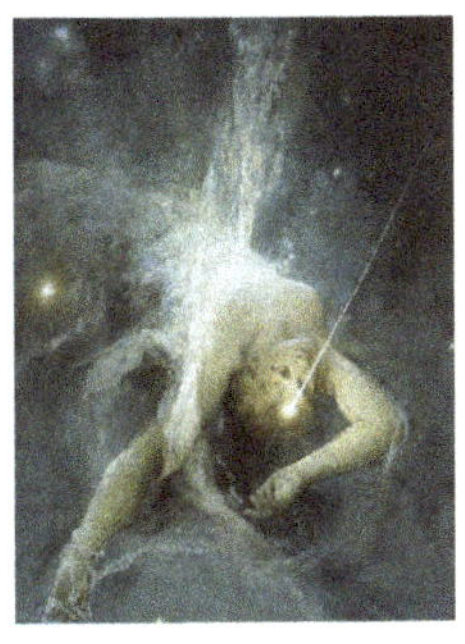

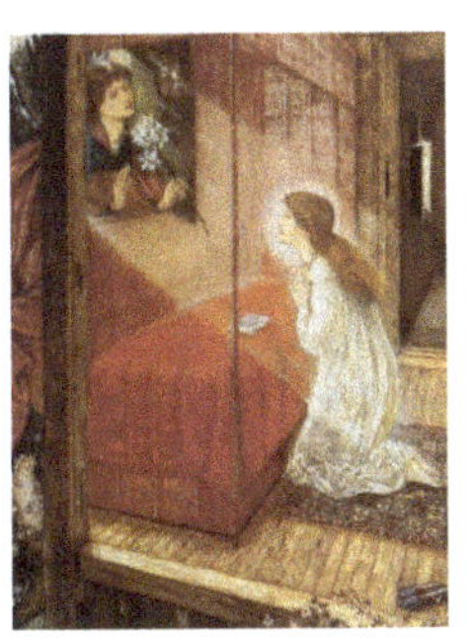

7 INTRODUCTION

19 MAJOR ARTISTS

    21 PIERRE PUVIS DE CHAVANNES

    25 ARNOLD BÖCKLIN

    29 GUSTAVE MOREAU

    33 DANTE GABRIEL ROSSETTI

    37 EDWARD BURNE-JONES

    41 ODILON REDON

    45 EUGÈNE CARRIÈRE

    49 MIKHAIL ALEKSANDROVICH VRUBEL

    51 FERNAND KHNOPFF

    55 JAN TOOROP

    57 EDVARD MUNCH

    61 FRANZ VON STUCK

    63 JENS FERDINAND WILLUMSEN

    65 MAURICE DENIS

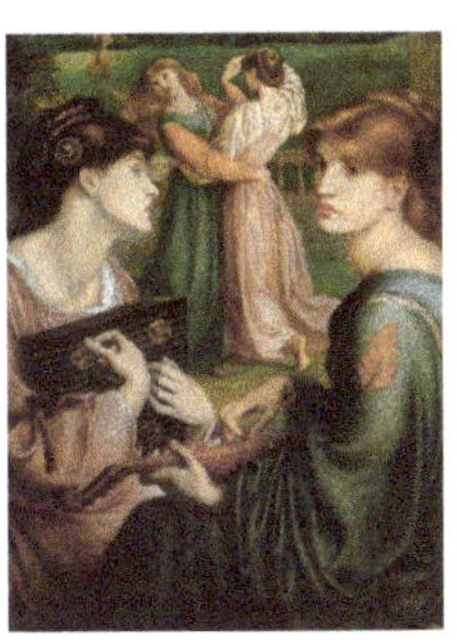

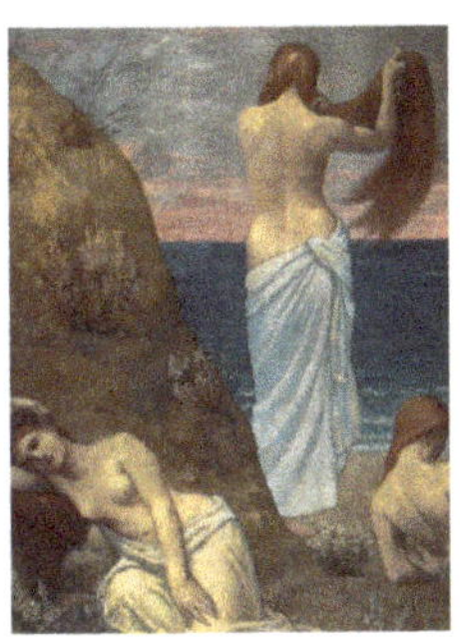

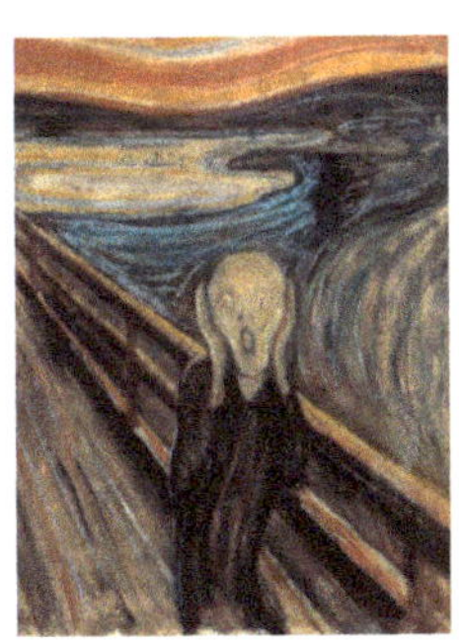

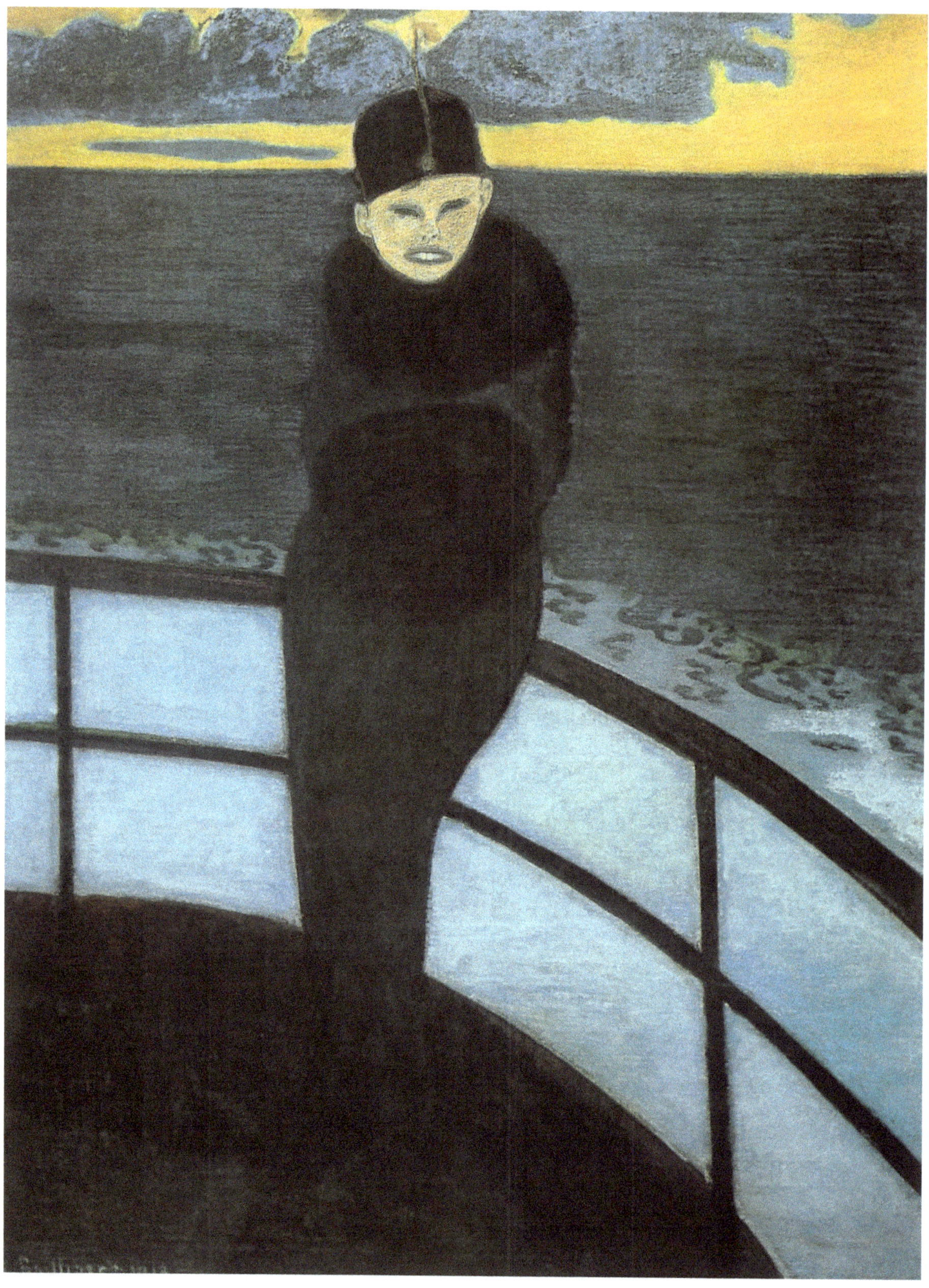

INTRODUCTION

With excerpts of The Manifesto of Symbolism by Jean Moréas:

Like all arts, literature evolves: a cyclical evolution with strictly determined turns which become complicated by various modifications brought about by the march of time and the upheavals of surroundings. It would be superfluous to point out that each new evolutionary phase of art corresponds exactly to senile decrepitude, to the inevitable end of the immediately previous school.

Every manifestation of art fatally manages to impoverish itself, to exhaust itself; then, from copy to copy, from imitation to imitation, what was once full of sap and freshness dries out and shrivels up; what was the new and spontaneous becomes the conventional and the cliché.

And so Romanticism, after having sounded every tumultuous alarm of revolt, after having had its days of glory and battle, lost its strength and its grace, abdicated its heroic audacities, made itself orderly, skeptical and full of good sense: in the honorable and paltry attempt of the Parnassians it hoped for deceptive revivals, then finally, like a monarch fallen in childhood, it let itself be deposed by Naturalism, to which one can only seriously grant a value of protest, legitimate but ill-advised, against the dullness of some then fashionable novelists.

A new manifestation of art, therefore, was expected, necessary, inevitable. This demonstration, incubated for a long time, has just hatched. And all insignificant anodynes of the joyful in the press, all the concerns of serious critics, all the bad temper of the public, surprised in its sheep-like nonchalance, only further affirm every day the vitality of the present evolution in French arts, this evolution noted in a hurry by judges, by an incredible discrepancy, of decadence.

▲ **Witold Pruszkowski**,
Falling Star, 1884.
Oil on canvas.
The National Museum, Warsaw.

◀ **Léon Spilliaert**,
The Crossing, 1913.
Pastel and coloured pencils, 90 x 70 cm.
Private collection.

It was mentioned at the beginning of this article that the evolution of art offers an extremely complicated cyclic character of divergences: thus, to follow the exact filiations of this new school, it would be necessary to go back to certain poems of Alfred de Vigny, back to Shakespeare, back to the mystics, further still. These questions would demand a whole volume of commentaries; therefore, let us say that Charles Baudelaire must be considered as the true precursor of the current movement; Stéphane Mallarmé allots to it the sense of mystery and the ineffable.

Baudelaire, the avant-courrier of the symbolists, was called "one of the curiosites romantiques." The poet of "Les Fleurs du Mal" loved what was improperly called "le style decadent," which is nothing more than an art arrived at the point of extreme maturity — an ingenious, complicated, learned style, full of shading and research, assimilating colors from all palettes, as well as notes from all key boards. It expresses new ideas in new forms, and in words not heard before. It was because of a strange fascination of the horrible, sickly, that the poet felt obliged to depict suffering humanity, but he has no abiding place there. He soars again to spiritual realms of the purest blue. As Théophile Gautier (1811 – 1872), the French art and literary critic says, *"If Baudelaire's bouquet is composed of strange flowers, metallic in color and peculiar in perfume, in the calix of which instead of dew are bitter tears, he will answer you. Undoubtedly roses and violets are more agreeable spring flowers, but they do not grow very well in the black mud of the pavements in a large city. This phase of life at once attracts and repels him; he acquires deep melancholy (for he judges himself no better than others), and he suffers at seeing the pure dome of the heavens and the chaste skies veiled by these poisonous vapors."*

A work of art connected to the ideas of Symbolism cannot be an object of calm, objective reading or contemplation. Alfred de Musset (1810 - 1857) wrote that Romanticism was everything that agitates and disturbs the soul – and the same can be said of Symbolism. Only in Symbolism there is also the presence of strangeness, and mystery, and the sensation of the other-worldly, and fear, and the feeling of doom.

This movement in European literature and art has been called by many names, "Decadence," "Symbolism," "Impressionism," none of them quite exactor comprehensive. What they seek is not general truth, but " la verité vraie," the very essence of truth. The symbolist would flash upon you the soul of that which can be apprehended only by the soul. The finer sense of things unseen, the deeper meaning of things evident.

Symbolism began as a literary movement, which appeared between the 1880s and 1900 among French poets, *les poètes maudits* (accursed poets), in particular with Charles Baudelaire's *Les Fleurs du mal* and flourished throughout Europe. It

Louis Welden Hawkins, ▶
The Halos, 1894.
Oil on canvas, 61 x 50 cm.
Private collection, Paris.

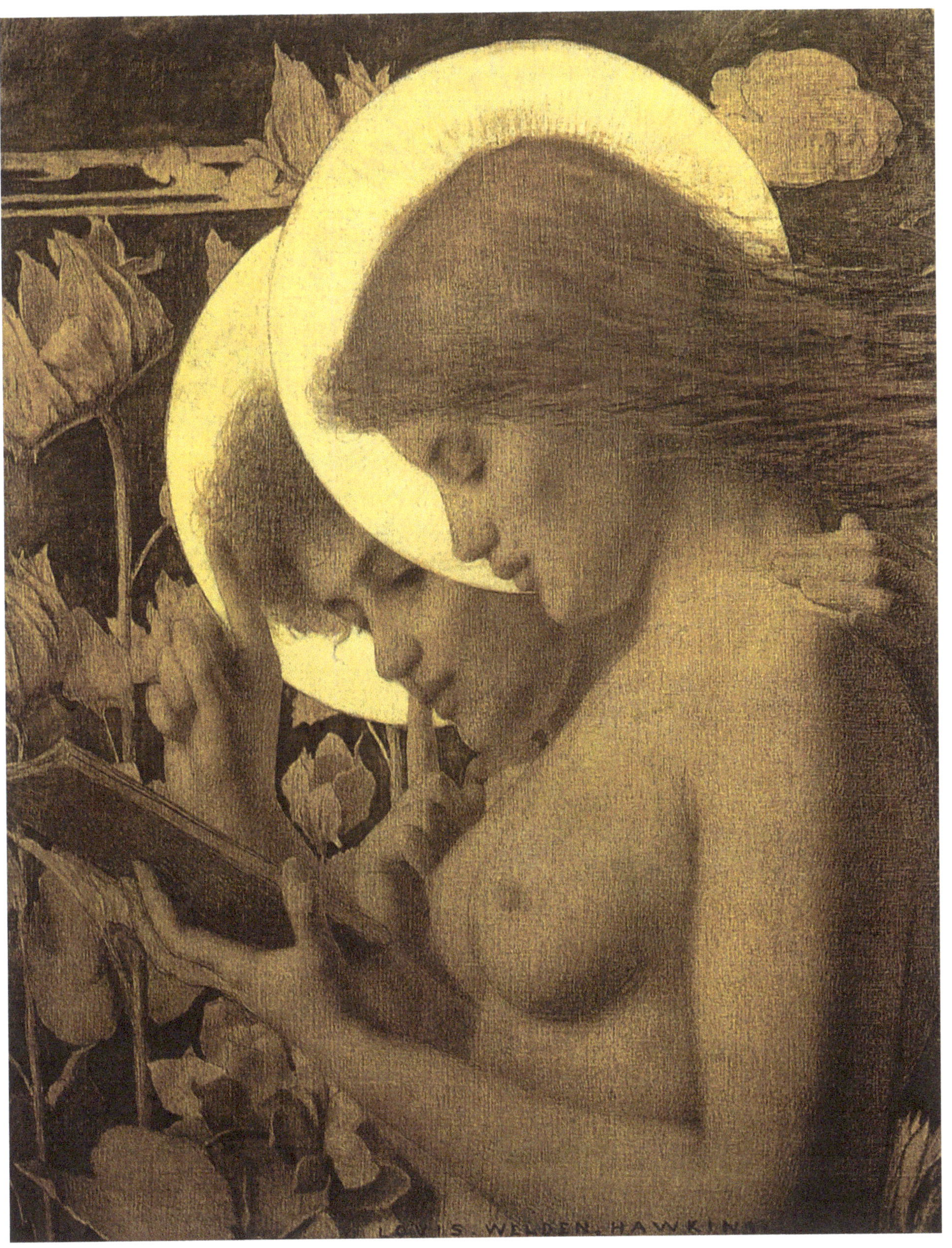

LOVIS WELDEN HAWKINS

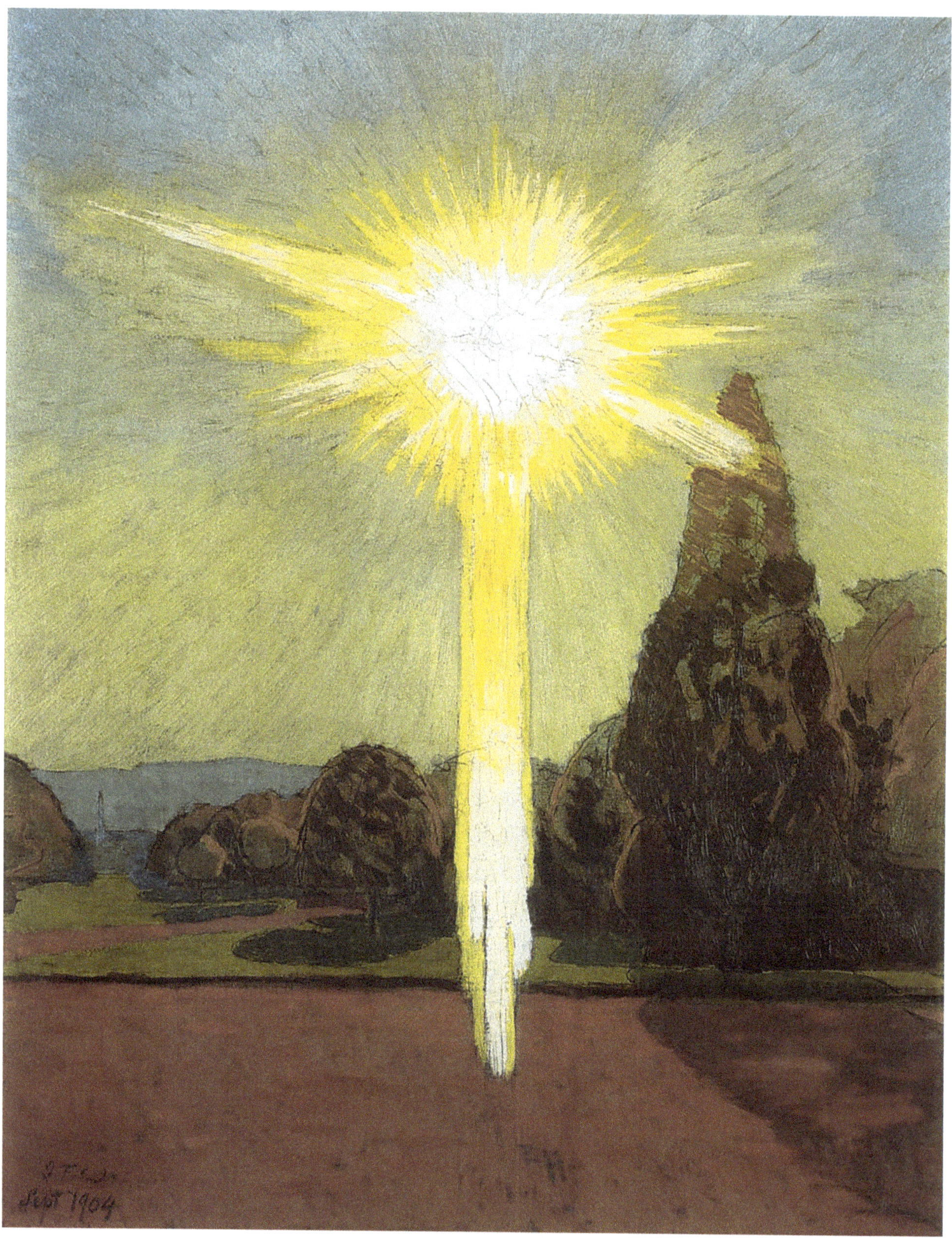

Sept 1904

began as a reaction to the literal representation of subjects preferring to create more suggestive and evocative works. The Symbolists sought a deeper reality from within their imagination, their dreams, and their unconscious; their common denominator is the emphasis on emotions, feelings, ideas, and subjectivity rather than realism.

To symbolize is to evoke, not to tell, narrate or paint. To suggest is its aim. For the exact translation of its synthesis it needs an arch-type, a complex form. *«Our expression is the symbol of our dream; our dream is the symbol of our thought,"* so says Charles Morice (1861-1919). We have already proposed the name of *Symbolism* as the only one capable of reasonably designating the present tendency of the creative spirit in art.

Remy de Gourmont (1858 – 1915), with literature in mind, said that Symbolism was anti-Naturalism. In this case, for painting, sculpture, and drawing, it is anti-Realism and anti-Impressionism. However, if Realism and Impressionism were the trends that possessed not only their ideas, but also their system of expressive means, Symbolism in the plastic arts was rather the reflection of a literary-intellectual movement. The ideas of Symbolism ruled over minds in the post-Impressionism epoch and came into the art of the most diverse

◀ **Jens Ferdinand Willumsen**,
Sun in the Park, 1904.
Oil and tempera on canvas, 194 x 169 cm.
J. F. Willumsens Museum, Frederikssund.

artists in their creative aspirations. The great visionaries, those whose hallucinations became the generalized expression of human emotions – the Spaniard Francisco de Goya (1746 – 1828), the Englishman William Blake (1757 – 1827), the Dutchman Jerome Bosch (1450 – 1516) and the Swiss Johann Heinrich Fuseli (1741 – 1825) – can be considered the Symbolists' teachers of the fine arts of the past. The symbolical and mystical tendency, however, which is represented by the decorative drawings of the Swiss Carloz Schwabe, is too foreign to the French spirit to allow us to consider these various artists as the genesis of a school: they are rather vestiges of the past.

The Symbolists' direct predecessors were the German Romanticists – Caspar David Friedrich (1774 – 1840), Philipp Otto Runge 1777 – 1810), Nazareans – a group of early 19th century German Romantic painters who aimed to revive honesty and spirituality in Christian art and the English Pre-Raphaelites. The symbolists in France have accomplished, up to a point, a task which is analogous to that of the English Pre-Raphaelites, or at least some of them, notably of Dante Gabriel Rossetti (1828 – 1882), George Frederic Watts (1817 – 1904) and Edward Burne-Jones 1833 – 1904).

The movement has been a protest simultaneously against the School and against Realism. The two great French symbolist painters, Gustave Moreau and Pierre Puvis de Chavannes, immediately recognized Burne-Jones as an artistic fellow traveler. But, it is very unlikely that Burne-Jones would have accepted or even, perhaps, have understood the label of 'symbolist'. Yet he seems to have been one of the most representative figures of the symbolist movement and of that pervasive mood termed "fin-de-siecle".

At the close of the nineteenth century in Europe there were scores of artists who connected their work with the ideas, symbols, figurative patterns, and topics of literary Symbolism. In Germany, they were called "late Romantics" – Arnold Böcklin (1827 – 1901) with his symphonies of color, Hans von Marees, (1837 – 1887) Hans Thoma (1834 – 1924) and Franz von Stuck (1863 – 1928). In Belgium, among the whole group of artist-Symbolists, Fernand Khnopff (1858 – 1921) stood out; in Norway, with the ecstatically turbulent style of Edvard Munch (1863 – 1944), in Russia, Mikhail Vrubel (1856 – 1910) and in Switzerland, Ferdinand Hodler (1853 – 1910).

Since the mid-19th century, the color white had occupied a symbolic place, in literature with Poe (1809 – 1849), Melville (1819 – 1891), and Mallarmé (1819 – 1891) and in art, for example, with Munch, Hodler, Kandinsky (1866 - 1944, or Malevich. White has often been connected with the search for the rudimentary, the primordial. The symbolical and mystical tendency was represented by the decorative drawings of the Swiss Carlos Schwabe (1866 – 1926). Among Symbolists there were those who created and expressed the brightest of all the new decorative styles of the end of the nineteenth century, which was called differently in different countries: in France *Art nouveau*, in Germany *Jugendstil*, in

Russia *modern style*. In England, for example, the protest of the painters against science and its industrial aspects will, under the influence of Ruskin (1819 – 1900), assume an abstract and literary character, which will cause it to misunderstand and forget painting for a certain period of time.

Symbolism is one of the most important aspects of the spiritual longing at the turn of the century in Russia. It is a logical development of Russian culture, not of a decadent atmosphere as in some western countries. Russian Symbolism strove to integrate beauty as a life-giving force into daily life. This was accompanied by a feverish search for the purpose of life after ethical ideals in the background of the impending collapse of old Russia. In contrast to the West, the expressiveness of Russian Symbolism extended until around 1910. The most brilliant of the Symbolists was Mikhail Vrubel. He created highly psychological portraits, linking the finest lyrical moments with expressive emotions and tragic loneliness. His worldview was imbued with a strange duality. He venerated Goethe and natural philosophy, and internalized the theories of Kant, Nietzsche and Schopenhauer.

The decorative manner of work by the Englishman Aubrey Beardsley (1872 – 1898), the Austrian Gustav Klimt (1862 – 1918), the Czech Alfonse

Carlos Schwabe, ▶
Sadness, 1893.
Oil on canvas, 155 x 104 cm.
Musée d'Art et d'histoire, Geneva.

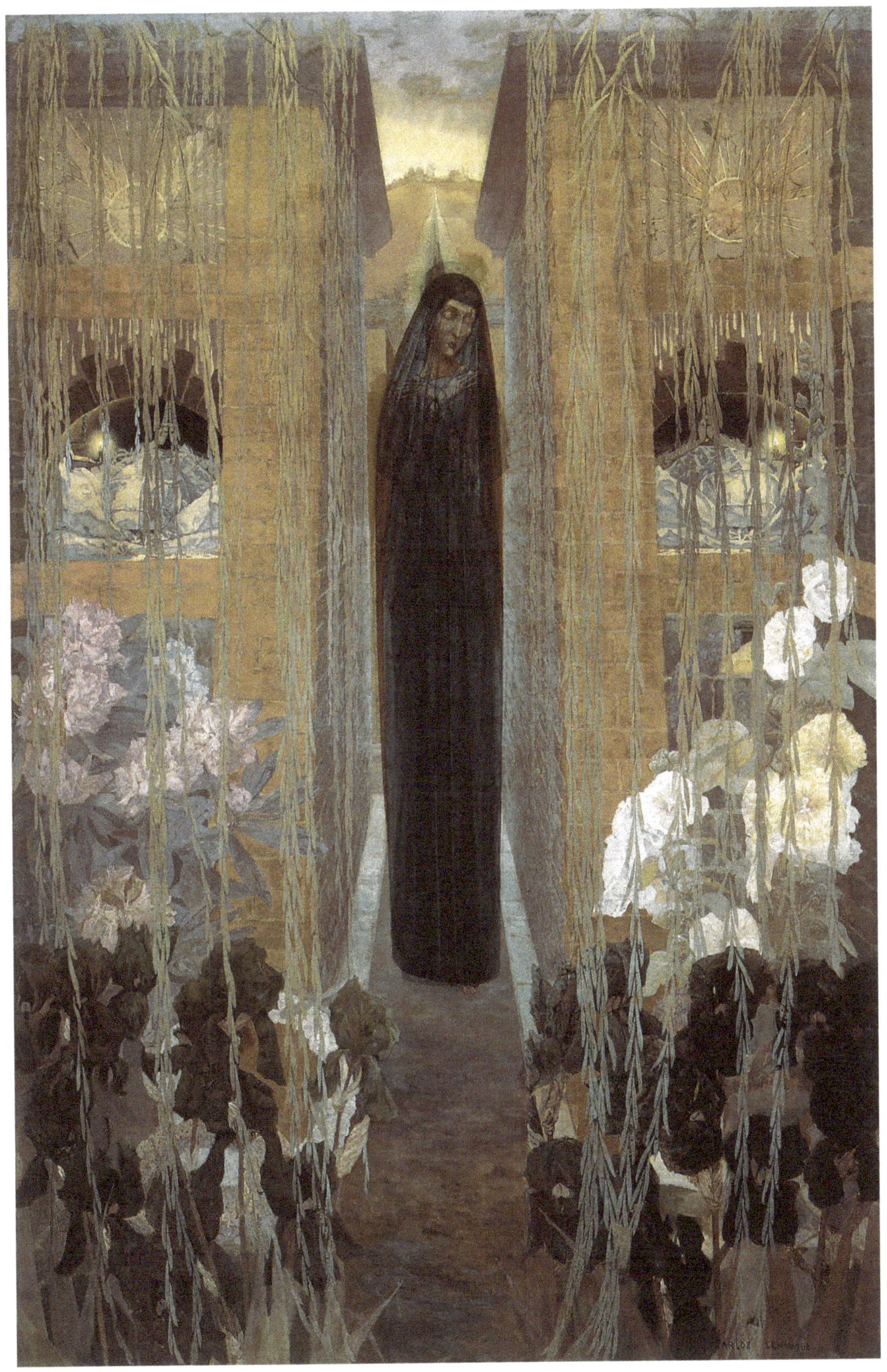

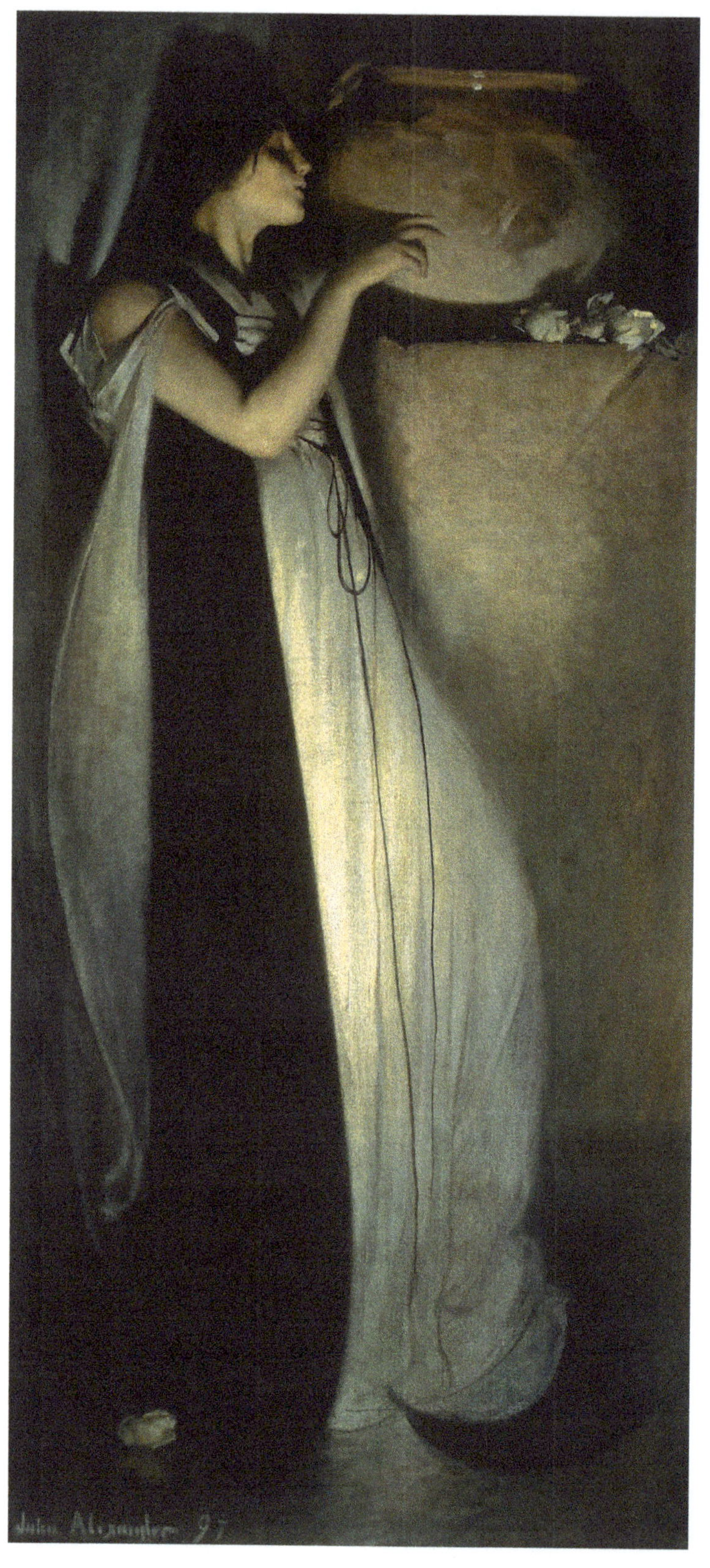

Mucha (1860 – 1939) and the Swiss Eugène Grasset (1845 – 1917) expressed the brightest of all this new style in drawing, posters and stained glass. Sometimes, the influences of Symbolism touched just casually some of the great masters whilst not becoming their main line of work – an example is Auguste Rodin (1840 – 1917).

In France, the motherland of Impressionism, Symbolism was first reflected in the plastic arts in the form of literary subject-matter. The idea of a painting based on a story was still very strong, despite the Impressionists' efforts to free painting from literature. The school, as in former times, graduated the ideally-prepared artist-artisans who created the masterpieces in the traditional classical manner and technique of painting. In the Salon, virtually the same as always, paintings whose subjects and characters had been taken from ancient mythology or Holy Scripture were exhibited every year. But now a tinge of mysticism, mystery, inexorable fate or melancholy appeared in them.

As before, they received Roman Prizes. Teachers like Cabanel (1823 – 1889), Baudry (1828 – 1886), Bouguereau (1825 – 1905), Bonnat (1833 – 1922) could still be proud of their disciples, now made fashionable with a touch of Symbolism. Albert Besnard received the most prestigious orders for wall-paintings – in Paris's *Hôtel de Ville*

◀ **John White Alexander,**
Isabel and the Pot of Basil, 1897.
Oil on canvas, 192.1 x 91.8 cm.
Museum of Fine Arts, Boston.

(town hall), in the Sorbonne, in the *Petit Palais* built for the World Exhibition of 1900. It had to come down to Albert Besnard (1849 – 1934) to meet with a real attempt at a Symbolism drawn from chemistry, electricity and the interpretation of science.

Georges Clairin (1943 – 1919) painted a group of secular portraits which struck one as real masterpieces. Henri Le Sidaner (1862 – 1939) and Henri Fantin-Latour (1836 – 1904) created easel paintings charming the spectator with tender sadness, the recollections of Wagner's images, mysterious visions. From 1892 to 1897 the new Salon that gathered young artists devoted to the ideas of Symbolism opened its doors six times. It was supported by Joseph Péladan, who went by the name of Sar Péladan, a member of the cabalistic Rosicrucian order. This order was based on the secret *Rosenkreutzer* societies of the eighteenth century, from which it preserved the interest in medieval Symbolism, alchemy, and esotericism. However, those artists for whom Symbolism represented something deeper than a literary topic, who came close to the expression of its ideas with the help of their painting, were never exhibited at Sar Péladan's.

The creator of monumental paintings, Pierre Puvis de Chavannes (1824 – 1898°), was capable of creating the sensation of mystery and dreaminess by means of the generalization of forms, light coloring and strangely immovable women's figures. A woman-myth, ideally beautiful and unreal – one of the most characteristic images in the painting of Symbolism – appears also in the paintings by Gustave Moreau, (1826 – 1928) for whom the power of painting consisted of color. His fairies, unicorns and mythical characters are born in the maelstrom of colors and in the contrasts of bright color, which makes them intriguing and enigmatic. Cabanel's disciple Eugène Carrière, on the contrary, leads one away into the realm of obscure visions by means of the toned manner of his painting. A simple color does not exist for him, he works by delicate transitions of tone that immerse his characters in the unreal, misty world of dreams.

And finally Odilon Redon, the only artist of the end of the nineteenth century who did not simply work in accordance with the spirit of the time, but was a true visionary. Although he studied under one of the most secular painters, Gérôme (1824 – 1904), lessons from the botanist Armand Clavaud (1828 – 1900), later assistant director of the "Jardin des Plantes" and the artist Bresdin (1822 – 1885), who created his own world of hallucinations in engraving, influenced Odilon Redon much more. The strange, sometimes monstrous, images of Redon's engravings, connected with animals and plants, are comparable only to Bosch's visions. The color in his paintings sometimes melts into soft, misty transitions from one area of the spectrum to another, sometimes almost scares by strange contrasts in the bouquets of simple wild flowers. Redon's Symbolism was spontaneous and direct and his work impressed his young contemporaries the most. Paul Gauguin (1848 – 1903) remembered Redon in his letters from Pacific islands, and Maurice

Denis portrayed him as the Teacher in the group of his friends the Nabis in the 1900 painting *Dedication to Cézanne*.

In the article *Paul: Symbolism in Painting* published in March 1891 in *Mercury de France*, the poet-Symbolist and critic Albert Aurier (1865 – 1892) tried to formulate the basic laws of the art of Symbolism. He counted five elements characteristic of literature as well as of painting. Three of them – moral intelligence, symbolicalness, and subjectivity – are the principles of the very attitude of Symbolism. The other two – a synthetic quality and decorativeness – concern directly the manner of expression in relation to painting and figurative language. Aurier said that a Symbolist should simplify the tracing of signs. Each of his contemporaries, due to the subjectivity of art declared by Symbolists, understood these laws in his own way; however, each, more or less, realized them in his creative work. Symbolism became that background on which the heterogeneous, contradictory art of the post-Impressionism epoch existed.

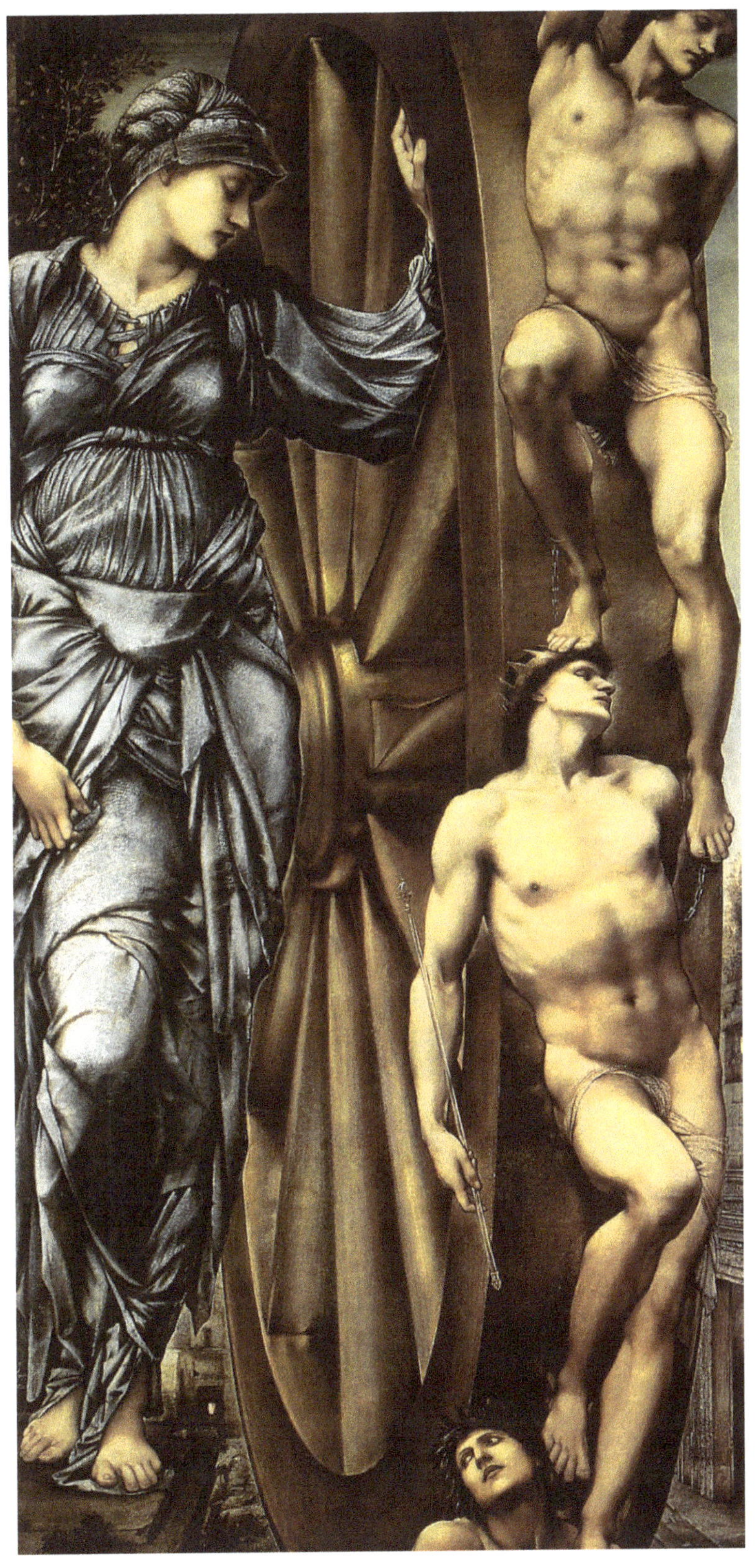

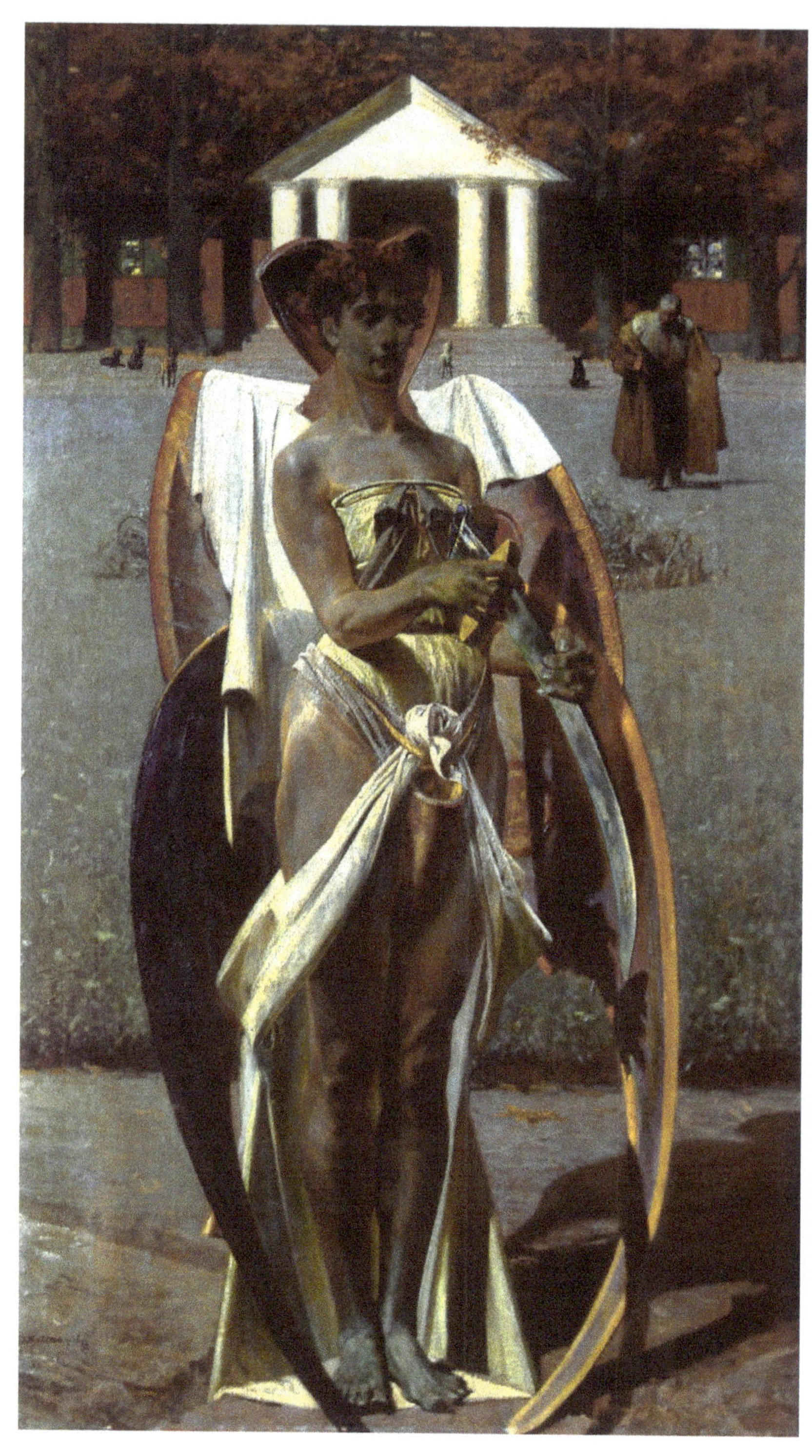

▲ **Jacek Malczewski**, *Thanatos I*, 1898.
Oil on canvas, 134 x 74 cm. The National Museum, Warsaw.

MAJOR ARTISTS

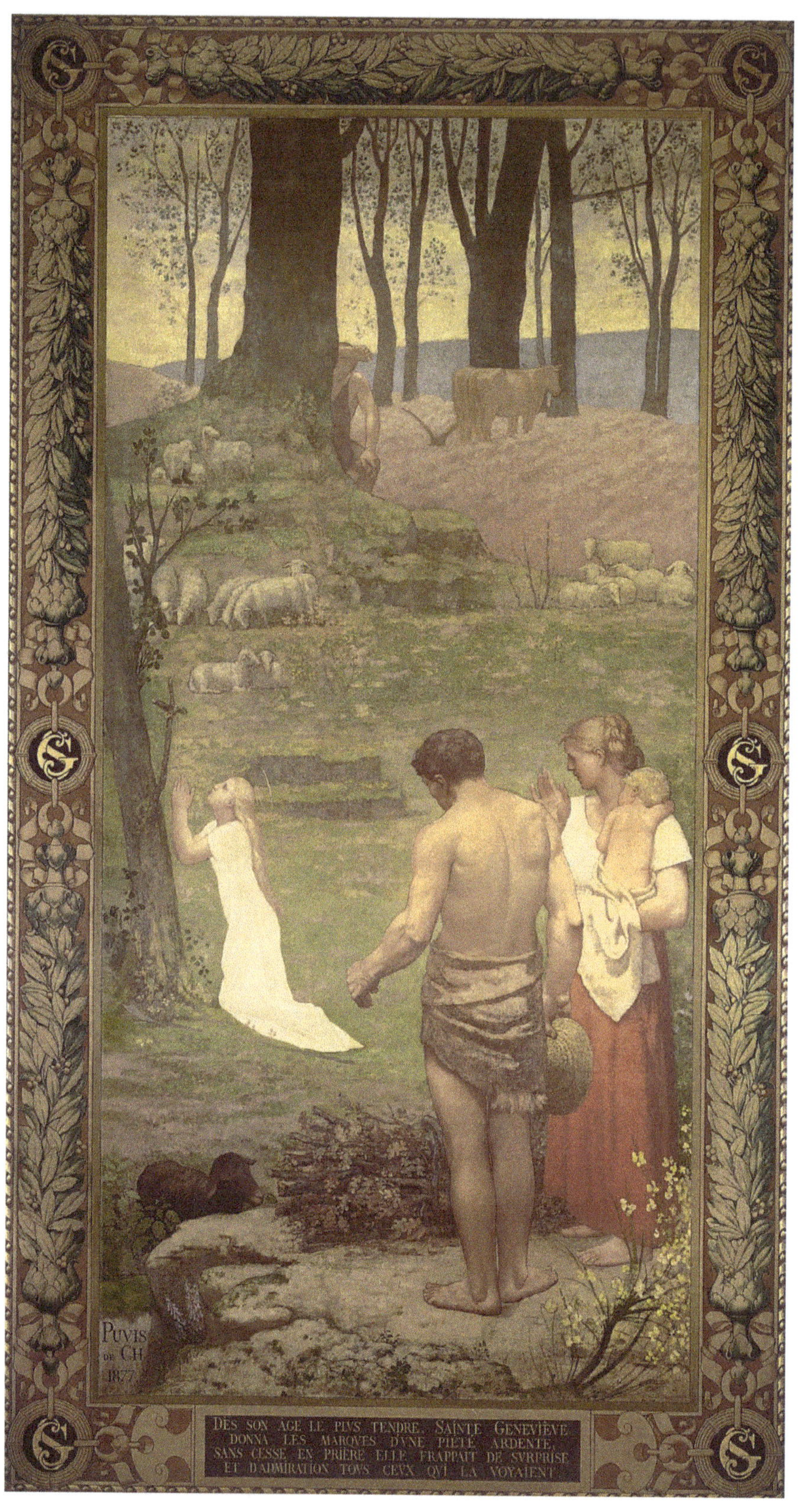

PVVIS
DE CH
1877
DES SON AGE LE PLVS TENDRE, SAINTE GENEVIÈVE
DONNA LES MARQVES D'VNE PIÉTÉ ARDENTE,
SANS CESSE EN PRIÈRE ELLE FRAPPAIT DE SVRPRISE
ET D'ADMIRATION TOVS CEVX QVI LA VOYAIENT

Pierre Puvis de Chavannes

(Lyon, 1824 – Paris, 1898)

Puvis de Chavannes came from an aristocratic family. His father was an engineer of bridges and roads in Lyon (a member of the French corps of engineers called *Ponts et Chaussées*), and, after receiving a classical and mathematical education, Puvis de Chavannes proceeded to the Polytechnic in Paris to adopt his father's profession.

Born in Lyon, Pierre Cécile Puvis de Chavannes took up painting rather late in life. It was not until he was thirty-five that some vacant panels in his brother's new house drew his attention to mural decoration As a member of a distinguished family he studied literature and mathematics before entering the *Ecole Polytechnique* in Paris with the intention of pursuing a career in his father's footsteps.

Puvis was apparently standing before the still-blank walls of his father's house when he experienced an artistic awakening and discovered he had a remarkable talent for wall decoration. He made an enlarged copy of one of his drawings and sent it to the Salon. Its

acceptance encouraged him to go on in the same vein and that was the beginning of his public career as a mural painter. Henceforth determined to devote himself to painting, he studied with Eugène Delacroix and Thomas Couture. An enlargement of one of his drawings appeared in the Salon of 1850, but several subsequent Salons rejected him.

Puvis' skill for color is manifested particularly in the landscape parts. He selected for the sky a tone of blue that has more light in it than the greens of the earth, and varied the tones of the latter by almost imperceptible gradations of light and less light tones. In this management of values and knowledge of forms and construction, he is the equal of the best landscape painters. While his landscapes give an impression of space and seem filled with air that surrounds the figures, they also give the impression of being flat to the wall until by a process of severely logical experiments he was able to depict not form, but its essence and abstract suggestion. The result is that his decorations do not impress upon us the idea of paint; they seem rather to have grown upon the wall like a delicate efflorescence.

◀ **Pierre Puvis de Chavannes**,
St Genevieve Child in Prayer, 1877.
Oil on canvas remounted on the wall, 462 x 221 cm.
Panthéon, Paris.

In 1881 Puvis completed *The Poor Fisherman* (*Pauvre Pêcheur)*, one of his most remarkable canvases, remarkable as much for its composition as for its mood, so intensely melancholy as to be almost disturbing. But Puvis achieved public recognition mainly through his fresco commissions, in particular for the Musée de Picardie in Amiens and the Pantheon and the Sorbonne in Paris.

On these gigantic supports the artist expressed the full range of his talent. When his work was unveiled to the public, uniquely-colored frescos of extreme softness and delicacy were revealed. More symbolic in form than in subject matter, the work had an aura of mystical timelessness that transported the viewer to a realm of ethereal tranquility. Although sometimes criticized for his pale tonalities, the artist's gift for color is fully evident to anyone who wishes to see it. For the skies of his landscapes he employed an intensely luminous blue to produce a contrast with the greens of the earth. By subtly varying the quality of light in this way, Puvis enlivened his work on a whole new level: his frescos appear to proliferate quite naturally over the wall, thereby avoiding the look of man-made artifacts. The painting was vigorous, transforming the banality of the wall into an abstract, subjective statement, the symbolic essence of the artist's work. In their conveyance of a sense of air and space surrounding the figures and animating the scenes, the landscapes of Puvis are on a par with those of the greatest landscape painters.

With its pure and timeless aesthetic, the painting of Puvis was admired by the Nabis group, including Maurice Denis, and also attracted the sympathy and respect of Symbolist poets Stéphane Mallarmé and Alfred de Jarry (1873 – 1907).

Puvis co-founded the "Société Nationale des Beaux-arts" in 1890 after a rift occurred within the Société des Artistes Français, and served as its chairman from 1891. At the time of his death in Paris on 24 October 1898, Puvis de Chavannes was considered one of the greatest artists of the century and was crowned in glory. Nowadays, however, he is today a little-known figure of 19th-century art.

Pierre Puvis de Chavannes, ▶
Young Girls at the Seaside, 1879.
Oil on canvas, 205 x 154 cm.
Musée d'Orsay, Paris.

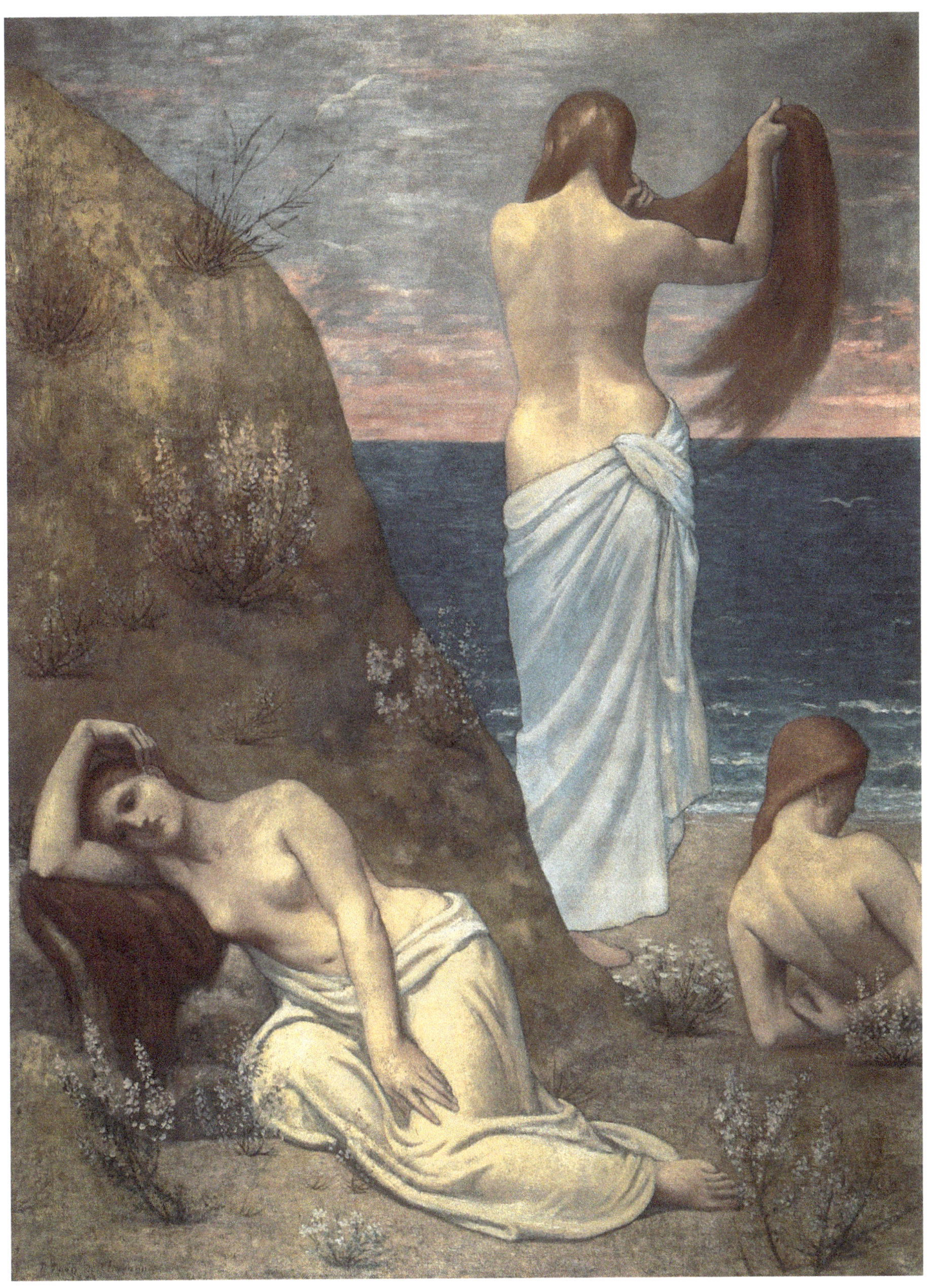

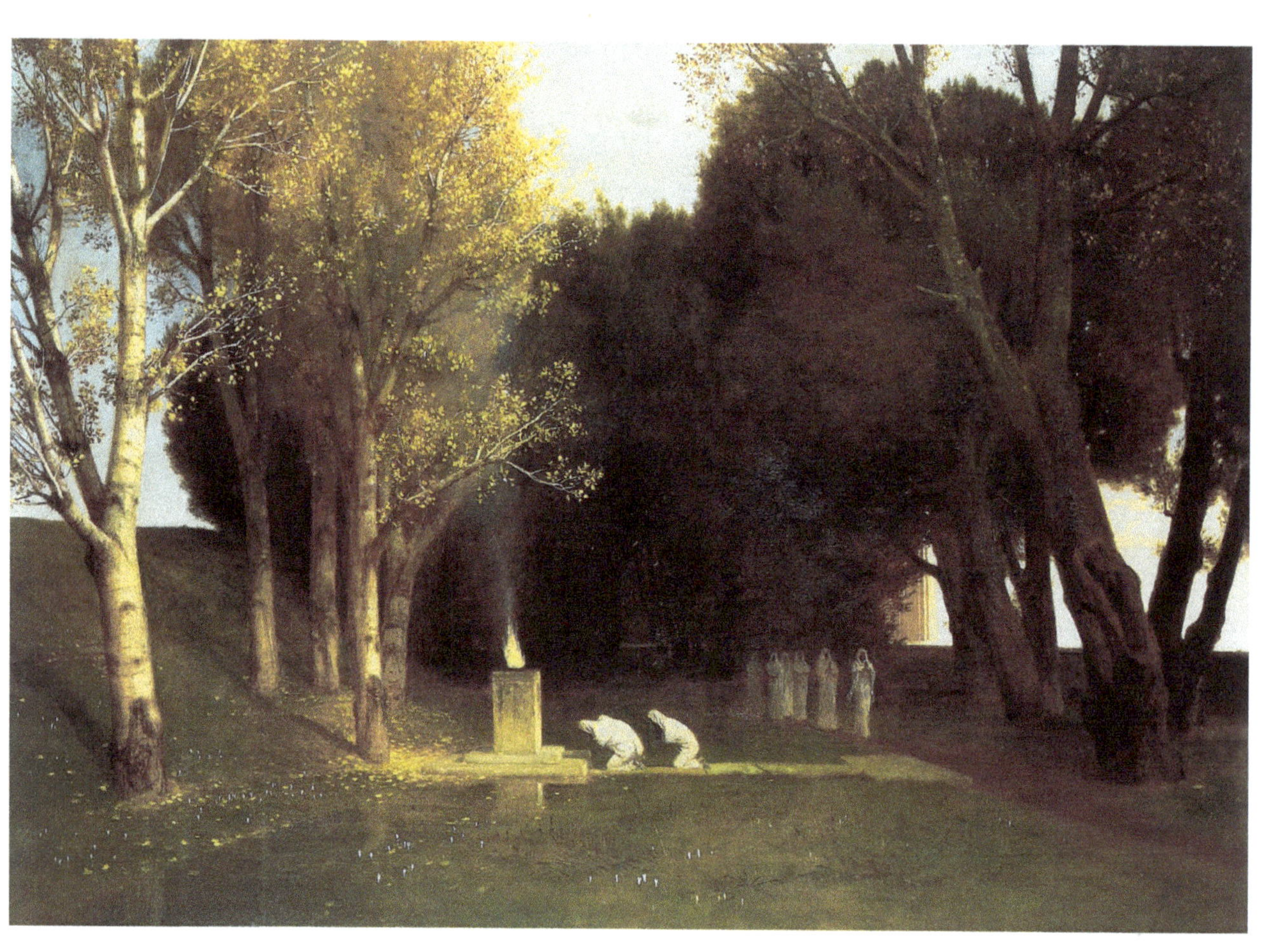

Arnold Böcklin

(Basle, 1827 – Zurich, 1901)

Arnold Böcklin is a major nineteenth-century artist who has been too-long forgotten. The son of a Swiss merchant was born in 1827 in Basle, Switzerland, *"one of the most prosaic towns in Europe".*

When he was nineteen years of age, he left Basle, the native place of another great painter, Holbein, and went to Düsseldorf to study at the Academy of Fine Arts, which he left in 1848 for two years' artistic wandering, during which he visited Antwerp, Brussels and Paris. He went to Rome in 1850. These biographical details indicate the development of Böcklin's talent, and it is not difficult to point out the different and distinct influences to which he was subject.

As German art preferred subject matter to artistic expression, these travels exposed Böcklin to a new concept of painting in which the artist was allowed to fully identify himself. In Italy he copied the old masters and developed his own highly-individual art, taking the Roman countryside as the inspiration for his many landscapes. Simultaneously majestic and sad, these works invariably provoke deep melancholy.

◀ **Arnold Böcklin,**
The Sacred Wood, 1882.
Varnished tempera on canvas, 105 x 150.5 cm.
Kunstmuseum, Basel.

Although traditional in his devotion to nature and his sense of expression, Böcklin also conveys a modern sensibility and spirit in his canvases. Setting his work in an intensely personal world where mythological creatures encounter the folklore of German mythology, Böcklin achieves a marvelous fusion of the sometimes conflicting trends of Naturalism and Expressionism. An inspired colorist, he went on to become a leading representative of the Symbolist movement. But like so many of his fellow artists, Böcklin was unappreciated during his lifetime. The proponents of modern art were shifting emphasis away from content towards form, even to the point of abstraction, and they deemed Böcklin's work overly narrative, despite its poignant Symbolism.

In 1880 Böcklin completed the first version of *The Island of the Dead*. Within six years he would complete five variations of this painting, now considered his most important work. A true masterpiece, the canvas has a moody ambiance that draws the viewer deep inside a dramatic setting that somehow manages to be both fantastical and real. The painting gives the viewer direct access to the painter's private world, a world that is simultaneously dreamy and melancholy.

A gifted colorist at a time when Richard Wagner was extracting sound colors out of music with

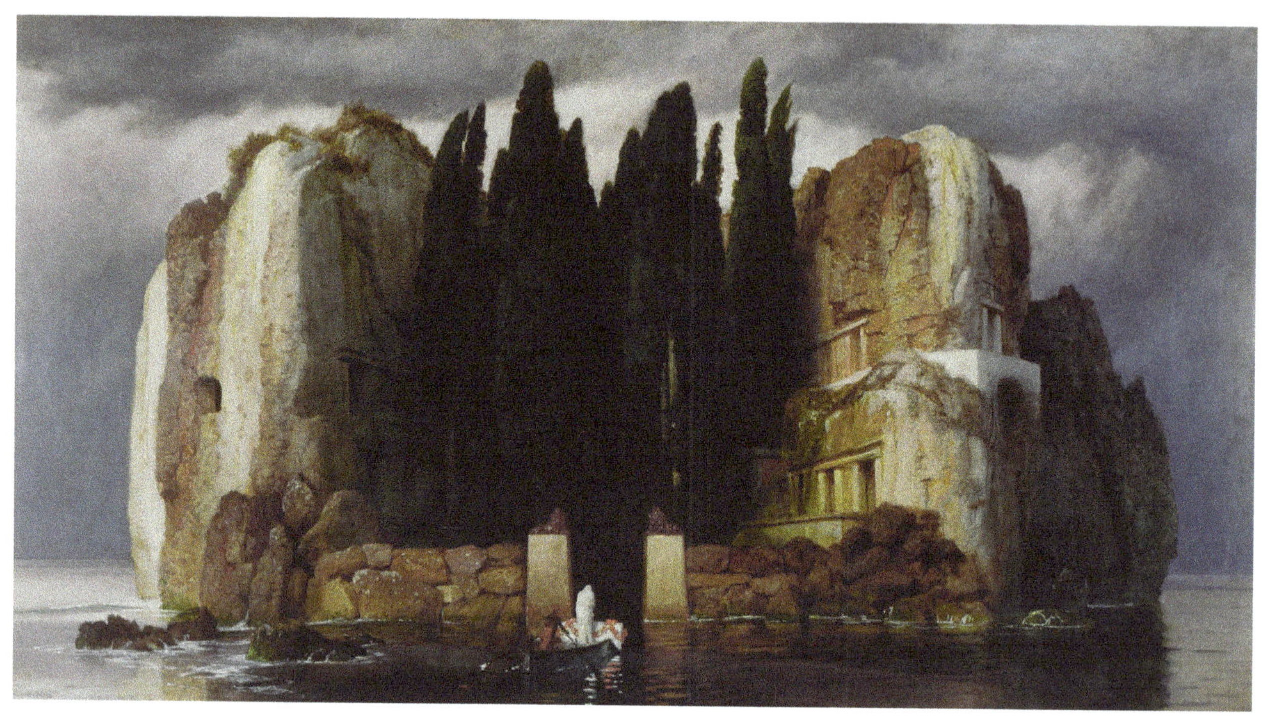

unprecedented brilliance, Böcklin's colors flowed over his canvases like the symphonic waves of an orchestra. With vivid colour that left viewers spellbound, the paintings became objects of bewitching splendour, and subsequent generations would honor Böcklin for being one of the most poetic colourists of the century.

In the 1920s Böcklin's work was rediscovered by the Surrealists, such as Giorgio De Chirico, Salvador Dalí, and Max Ernst. Regarding Böcklin as their predecessor, they hailed him as an "artistic genius", and found inspiration in the mythological visions, fantastic and iconoclastic, depicted on canvases populated by centaurs, naiads and other nymphs.

A modern man of culture would associate Böcklin's name with something great, surpassing the ordinary measure of things

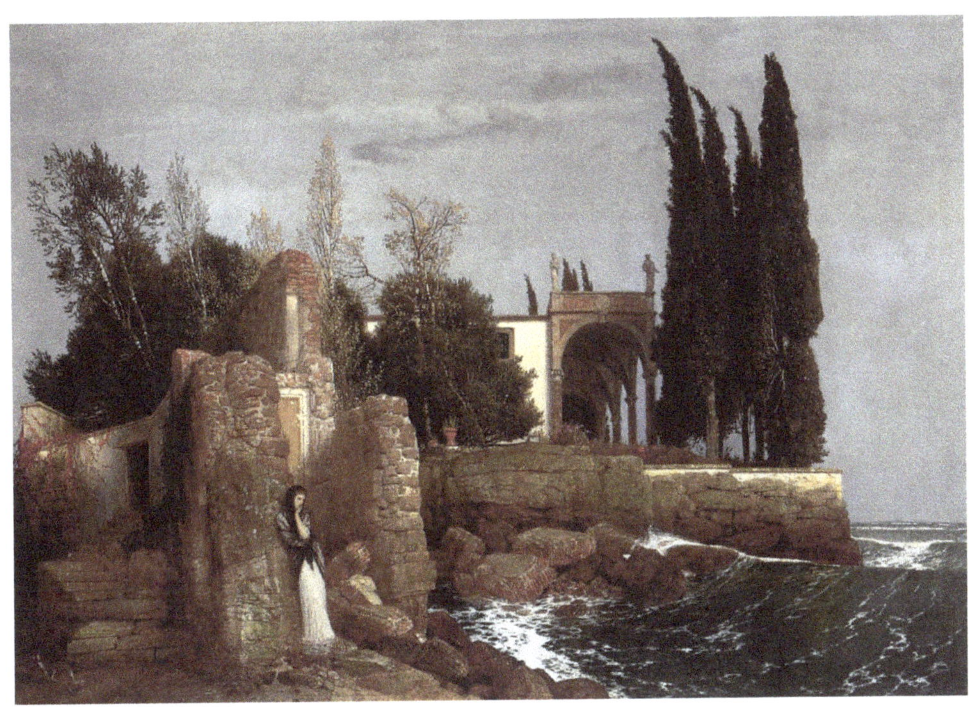

to which people are accustomed. Bocklin is a phenomenon, admired by all those who are able to understand him, he astonishes by the primitiveness of his nature, which resembles that of mythical people, and by his spiritual culture, which places him amongst the most eminent men of the nineteenth century.

In 2002 the Musée d'Orsay devoted an exhibition to the Swiss painter in the framework of its monograph series dedicated to rediscovering overlooked artists. Particularly well-timed to coincide with the artist's centenary, the exhibition gave the public (especially in France) an opportunity to rediscover Böcklin and allowed a re-evaluation of his work so that he could be restored to his rightful place within the history of modern art, namely as an artist whose œuvre is both singular and fundamentally Symbolist.

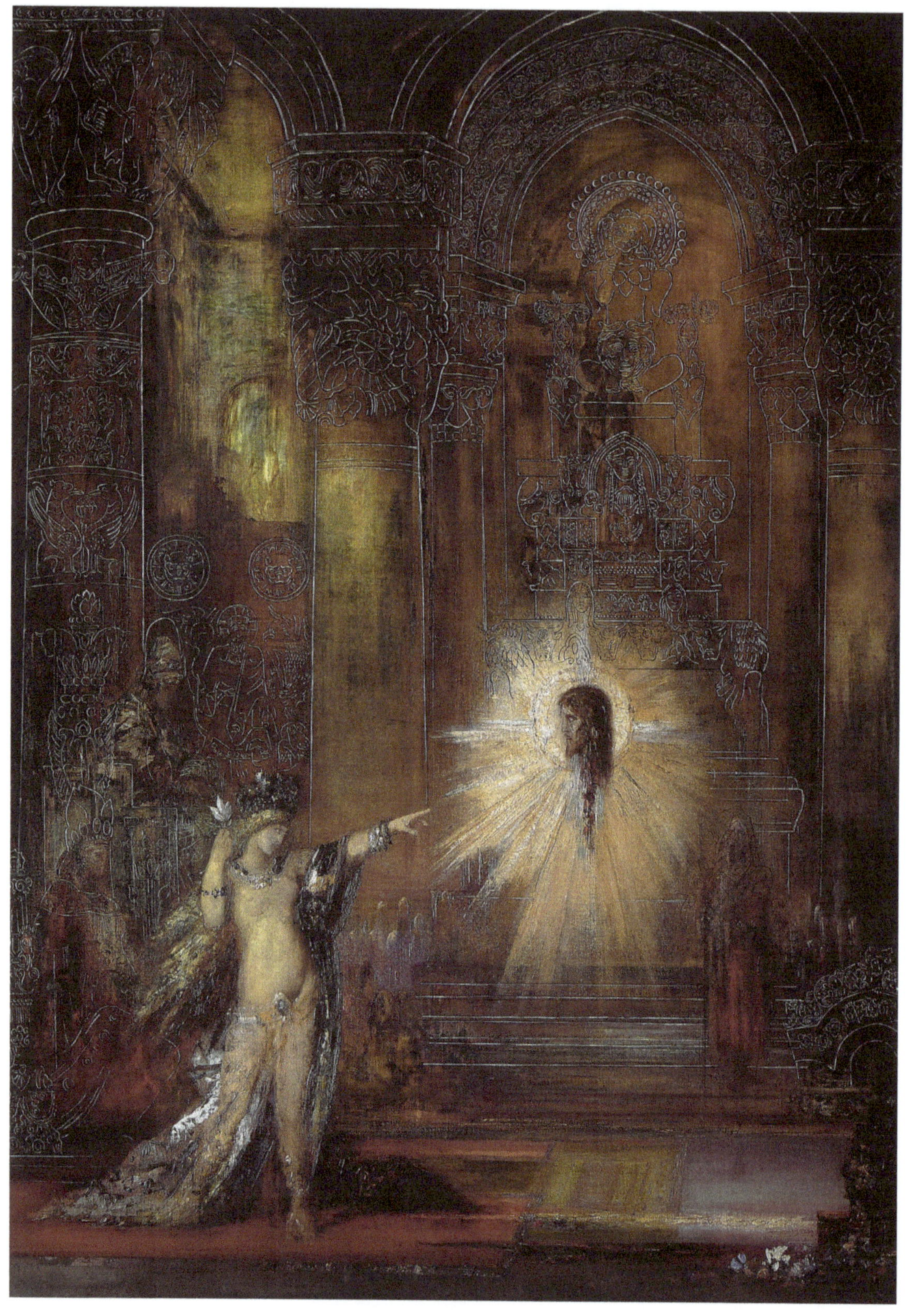

Gustave Moreau

(Paris, 1828 – Paris, 1898)

Acknowledged today as one of the greatest French Symbolist painters, Gustave Moreau was born in Paris in 1828. Exhibiting at the Salon, and later decorated with the French "Légion d'Honneur", Moreau's career unfolded primarily within the milieu of his native Paris.

As the son of an architect, Moreau was inculcated with a classical education at a very young age. He was only an eight-year-old boy when he started to develop the gifts that would make him a great draughtsman. Throughout his life he would collect drawings, copies, and photographs of works that he admired and which provided frequent inspiration.

After attending classes at Rollin College in Paris, Moreau made his first trip to Italy in 1841, filling a sketchbook with drawings in the process, and afterwards frequenting the private studio of the painter François-Edouard Picot, a decorator of public monuments and Parisian churches. These experiences made him a suitable applicant for admission to the "Ecole des Beaux-Arts" in Paris, to which he applied in 1846. He was admitted,

◀ **Gustave Moreau,**
The Apparition, 1876-1898.
Oil on canvas, 142 x 103 cm.
Musée national Gustave-Moreau, Paris.

but after a second failed attempt to win the « Prix de Rome », Moreau left the institution in 1849.

Retracing his travels in Italy, Moreau honed his knowledge of the Renaissance masters, including Veronese, Carpaccio, Raphael, and even Michelangelo, whose Sistine Chapel frescos Moreau spent hours copying. In Paris, Moreau likewise continued to apply himself by copying the Old Masters at the Louvre, and his work soon reflected the diversity of his many influences and indirect inspirations.

But it was his encounter with Théodore Chassériau (1819 – 1856) in 1851 that would ultimately empower Moreau's work. Impressed by the work of this famous student of Ingres, Moreau borrowed the intensity of Chassériau's tones, in particular the depth of his browns and reds. Through the vibrancy of their now incomparable colors, Moreau's canvases, always brilliantly handled, were saturated with a highly personal Symbolism that immersed the viewer in a fantasy world where dreams and mythology were always intersecting.

When he exhibited *Oedipus and the Sphinx (Œdipe et le Sphinx)* at the Salon of 1864, Moreau was harshly criticised by critics and the public alike, who were unable to see the winged creature,

John the Baptist that he depicted in levitation, rather than on a platter, caused a sensation. Moreau exhibited the painting that brought him to the public's attention once again at the 1878 Universal Exposition, but he was already widely considered an essential representative of French Symbolism.

In 1888 he was elected to the « Académie des beaux-arts », then appointed professor at the "Ecole des Beaux-Arts" in 1892.

Gustave Moreau died in Paris in 1898. A renowned painter, he died having achieved a late masterpiece when several years earlier he had applied the last stroke to *Jupiter and Semele (Jupiter et Semélé)*. If one canvas could possibly encapsulate the great Symbolist's entire *oeuvre*, it would be this one, for its intensity, its influences, and its heightened sense of detail.

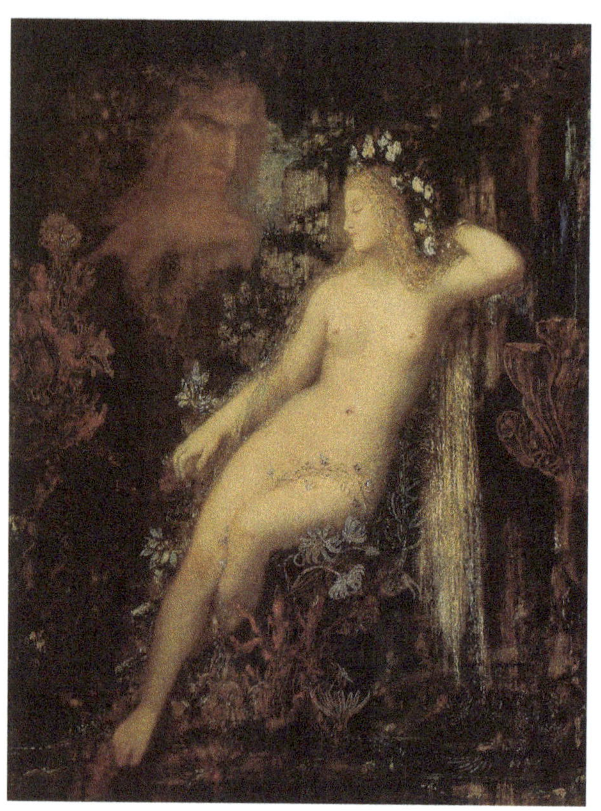

▲ **Gustave Moreau**,
Galatea, 1880.
Oil on wood panel, 85 x 67 cm.
Musée d'Orsay, Paris.

simultaneously wild and wise, as a powerful example of a purely symbolic art.

A visionary artist, Moreau had to wait twelve years for his work to be universally recognized. It was in 1876, when he offered Salon goers *The Apparition (L'Apparition)* that the public and critics finally opened their eyes to the beauty of his work. The head of Moreau's St

Gustave Moreau, ▶
Œdipus and the Sphinx, 1864.
Oil on canvas, 206.4 x 104.8 cm.
The Metropolitan Museum of Art, New York.

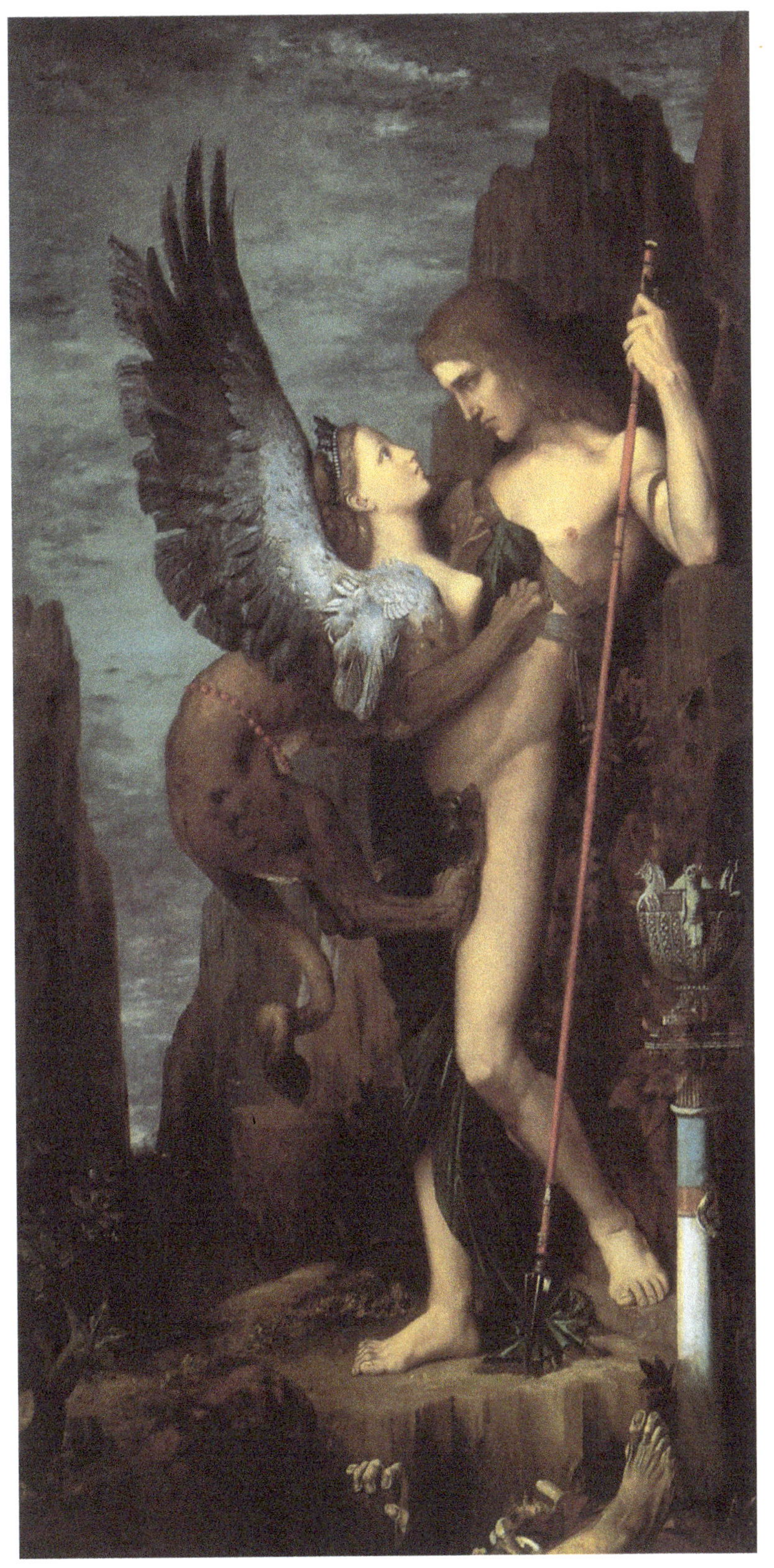

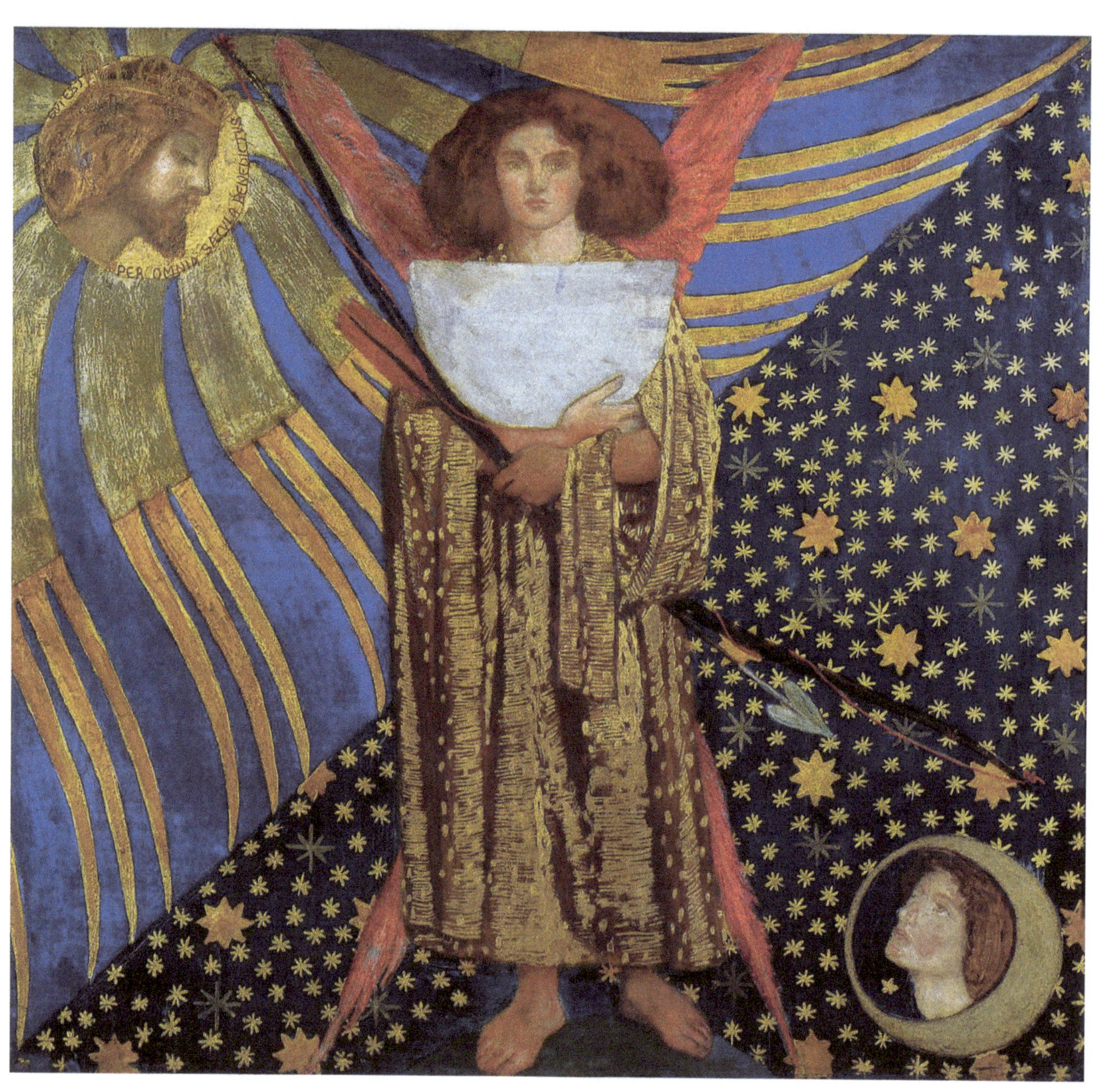

▲ **Dante Gabriel Rossetti,**
Dantis Amor, 1860.
Oil on mahogany, 74.9 x 81.3 cm.
Tate Gallery, London.

Dante Gabriel Rossetti

(London, 1828 – Birchington-on-Sea, 1882)

Both painter and a poet, Dante Gabriel Rossetti founded the Pre-Raphaelite brotherhood in 1848, along with the critic Leigh Hunt and the painters Holman Hunt and Sir John Everett Millais. The Pre-Raphaelites crossed the plastic arts with literature and religion, but there was no limit to their aesthetic goals beyond this union. Whereas Millais and Hunt preferred to adapt the drama of real events unfolding among men and women in a naturalistic world, Rossetti was more traditional, focusing on the depiction of scenes from the Bible and literary themes, in particular from Dante, Shakespeare, Goethe, and Edgar Allan Poe.

At the same time, Rossetti worked alongside Edward Burne-Jones and William Morris, and his works were greatly admired by John Ruskin. Passionate about drawing and writing, Rossetti combined his two interests in his canvases, where words often found a place.

In what would soon become a characteristic of the Pre-Raphaelite movement, Rossetti painted slowly, always concentrating on best representing the slightest detail naturalistically. Romantic in spirit, Rossetti translated the love affairs he experienced over the course of his life into his paintings. Elizabeth Siddal, whom he would marry in 1860, haunted his works until he met Jane Burden. Although Burden ended up marrying William Morris, she remained the true Pre-Raphaelite archetype of feminine beauty to Rossetti, who loved her for the rest of his life.

Settled in Oxford, Rossetti neglected and abandoned his wife. As neither partner had much money, Rossetti chose to rely on the favors of other women. The health of his wife, known as Lizzie, declined after a stillbirth and she ended her own life with an overdose of laudanum while still quite young, only two years after the marriage. This drama had a profound effect on Rossetti, both in his art and his person. Living in Chelsea afterwards, no doubt to escape unbearable memories, Rossetti expressed his feelings for his dead wife in his paintings, and continued to paint female models in works that combined a dangerous sensuality with deep melancholy. In 1864 he started work on *Beata Beatrix*. Full of Symbolism, this work, which he labored over for six years, is a true homage to his departed wife, perhaps in the spirit of redemption. During the final years of his life Rossetti fell into a deep depression and shut himself off in a macabre solitude. With his poetry under fierce attack by the critics, he stopped writing and buried his texts in Lizzie's grave. Having become paranoid, especially after being publicly attacked in the pamphlet *The Fleshy School of Poetry*, he stopped seeing his friends, in particular Ruskin, and only communicated by letter with a select few, including Jane Morris. Consumed by alcohol and drugs, Rossetti died in 1882. Forever torn between his two passions of painting and writing and destroyed by his own demons, Rossetti lacked the necessary fortitude to become a true master of either specialty, but nevertheless remains a major avant-garde artist of nineteenth-century England.

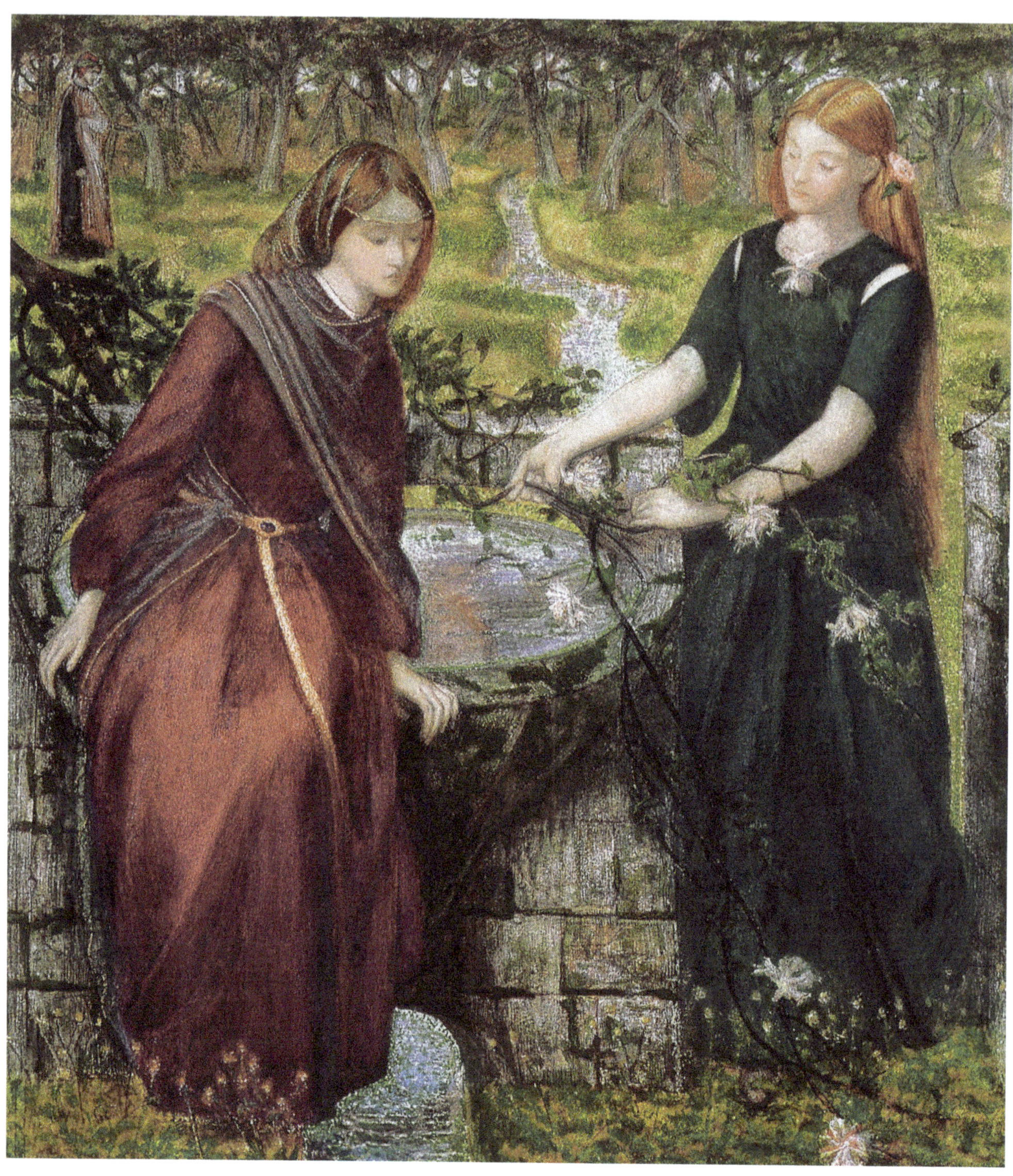

▲ **Dante Gabriel Rossetti,**
Dante's Vision of Rachel and Leah, 1855.
Watercolour on paper, 35.2 x 31.4 cm.
Tate Gallery, London.

Dante Gabriel Rossetti, ▶
The Bower Meadow, 1850-1872.
Oil on canvas, 86.3 x 68 cm.
Manchester Art Gallery, Manchester.

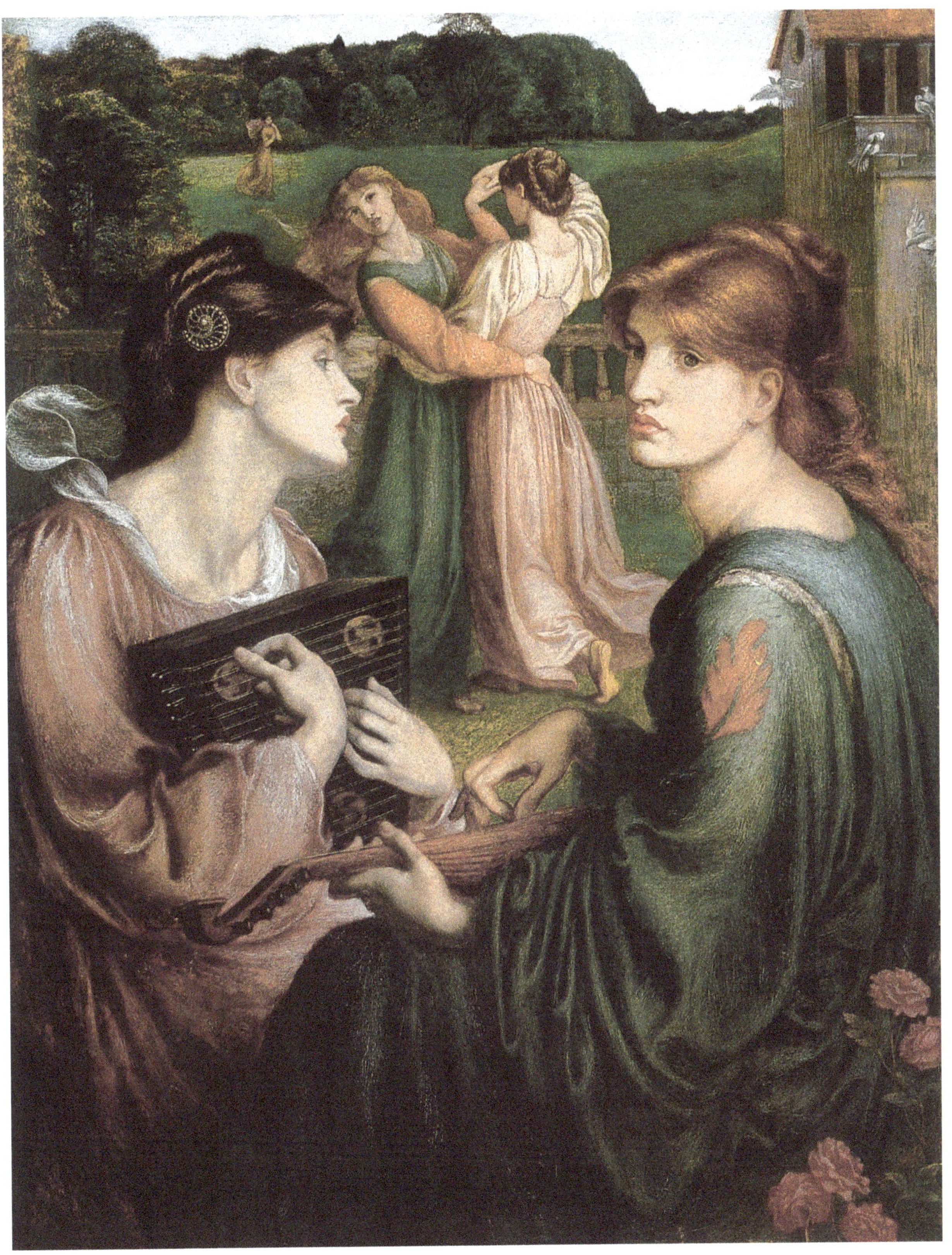

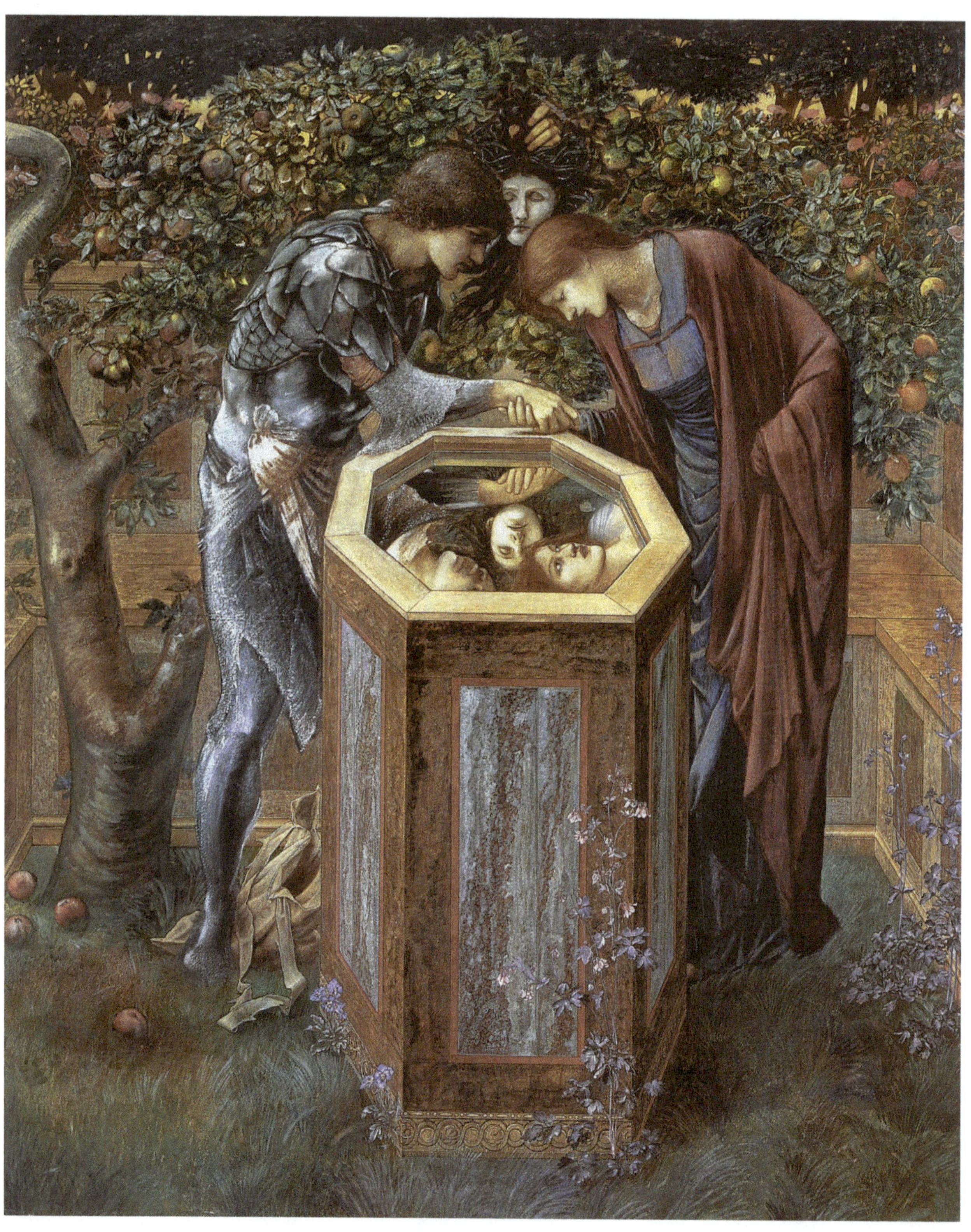

Edward Burne-Jones

(Birmingham, 1833 – London, 1898)

An almost self-taught painter who received only a few drawing lessons from Dante Gabriel Rossetti, Edward Burne-Jones was born in Birmingham in 1833. As his mother died several days after his birth, he was raised by his father in his native city. A brilliant student, at the age of twenty he left home to attend Exeter College, Oxford. There he met William Morris and two years later, having discovered the work of the painter and poet John Ruskin, the two friends went to live in London; Burne-Jones had decided to become a painter, Morris an architect.
In London Burne-Jones met Rossetti, with whom he became friends. In order to support himself, Burne-Jones worked at producing stained-glass window designs, in particular for the company founded by Morris called the Morris, Marshall, Faulkner & Co., later simply Morris & Co.

Taking his inspiration from Romantic literature, Burne-Jones started working on pencil and ink drawings and watercolours. He then made a new voyage to Italy, which he had previously discovered a few years earlier. Afterwards, inspired by these new perspectives, Burne-Jones, who had joined the brotherhood of the Pre-Raphaelites, produced a distinctive style. Combining Pre-Raphaelitism, Classicism, and Italian Primitivism, his work ultimately transcended all these influences in a subtle mixture of Romanticism and Symbolism.

Always looking for inspiration in literature, myths, and legends of primarily medieval origin, Burne-Jones applied himself particularly to the depiction of figures, which he often made from nature, and quickly became one of the most important painters of the Pre-Raphaelite movement. Accentuating the power of his images by making his canvases larger than convention dictated, Burne-Jones took great care to render the sensuality of the body and drapery in the Italian tradition. Spending a great deal of time painting his canvases, he often stopped work on one to begin work on another, or to take up where he had left off on an older work in order to finish it. Line and form took precedence over colour, and the tones of his canvases are often softened, sometimes resulting in a faded appearance that nevertheless always accentuates the melancholy, dreamlike quality of his work.

Acknowledged as a painter by his contemporaries, his reputation suffered a setback when he depicted Ovidian heroes in the nude in *Phyllis and Demophoon*. As a result of the harsh criticism this work received, Burne-Jones had to resign from

◄ **Edward Burne-Jones**,
The Baleful Head, 1885-1887.
Oil on canvas, 150 x 130 cm.
Staatsgalerie, Stuttgart.

the Old Watercolour Society he belonged to. His collectors, however, still held his work in high regard, and were able to maintain his reputation.

In 1889 Burne-Jones exhibited at the Universal Exposition in Paris, where his work was mostly well received by the public and where he won a first-prize medal. Acknowledged throughout Europe then as a major artist, he became a member of the "Académie royale de Peinture" in 1885, but resigned in 1893. Two years later he was knighted by Queen Victoria. Having become a major artist of his era, known throughout Europe, he died in London in 1898 as the greatest representative of the Pre-Raphaelite movement. The ultimate honor, which no other artist had previously received, was a memorial service held at Westminster Abbey at the request of the Prince of Wales, soon to become King Edward VIII.

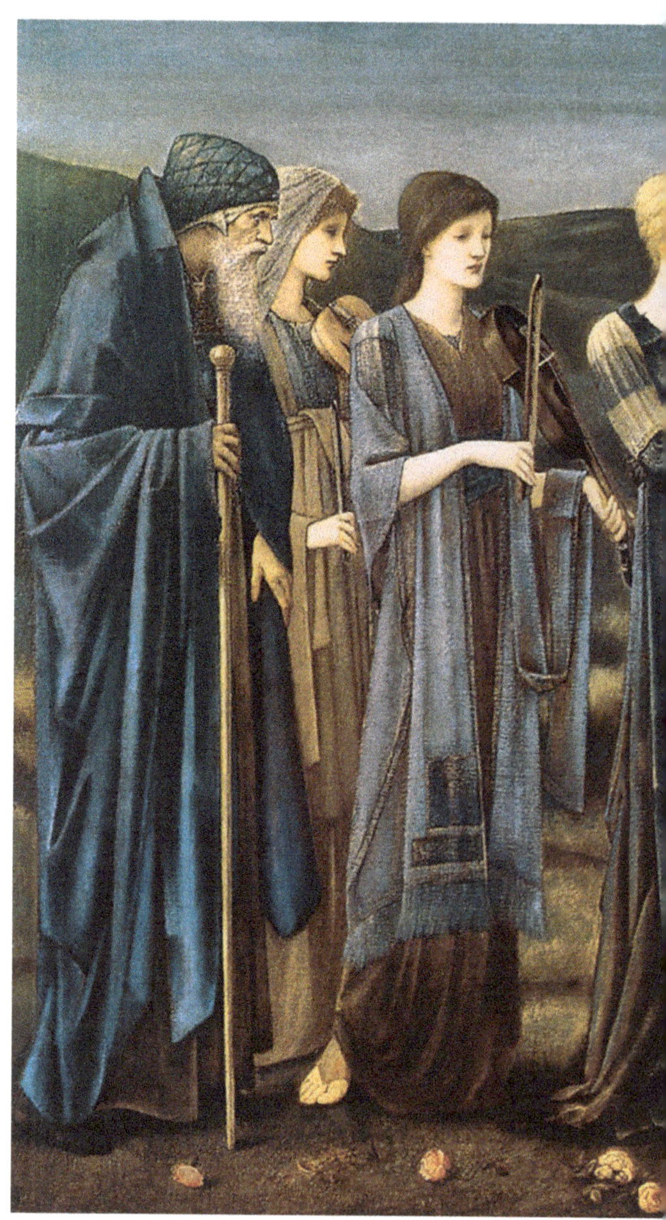

Edward Burne-Jones, ▶
The Wedding of Psyche, 1895.
Oil on canvas, 119.5 x 215.5 cm.
Musées royaux des Beaux-Arts de Belgique, Brussels.

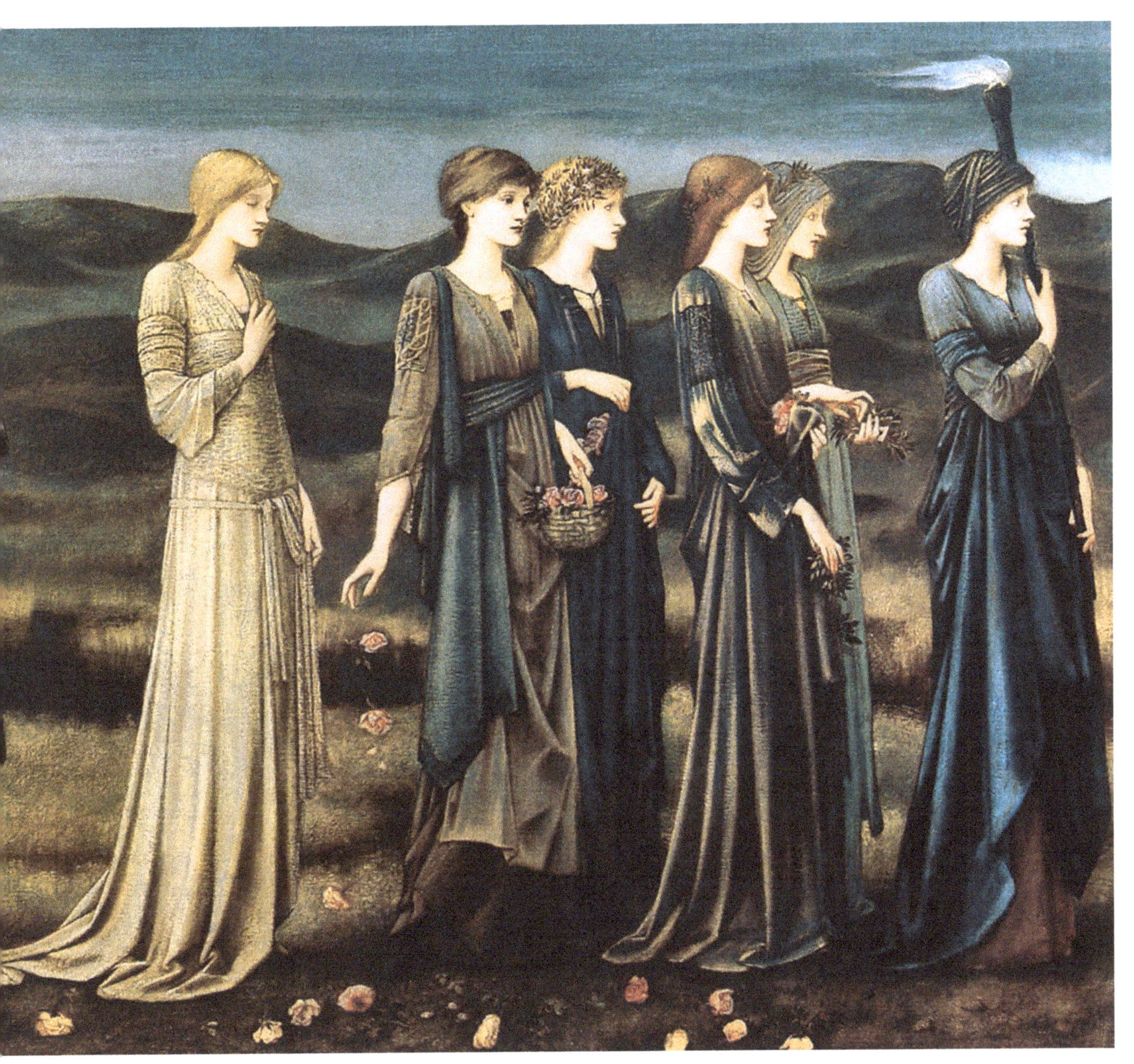

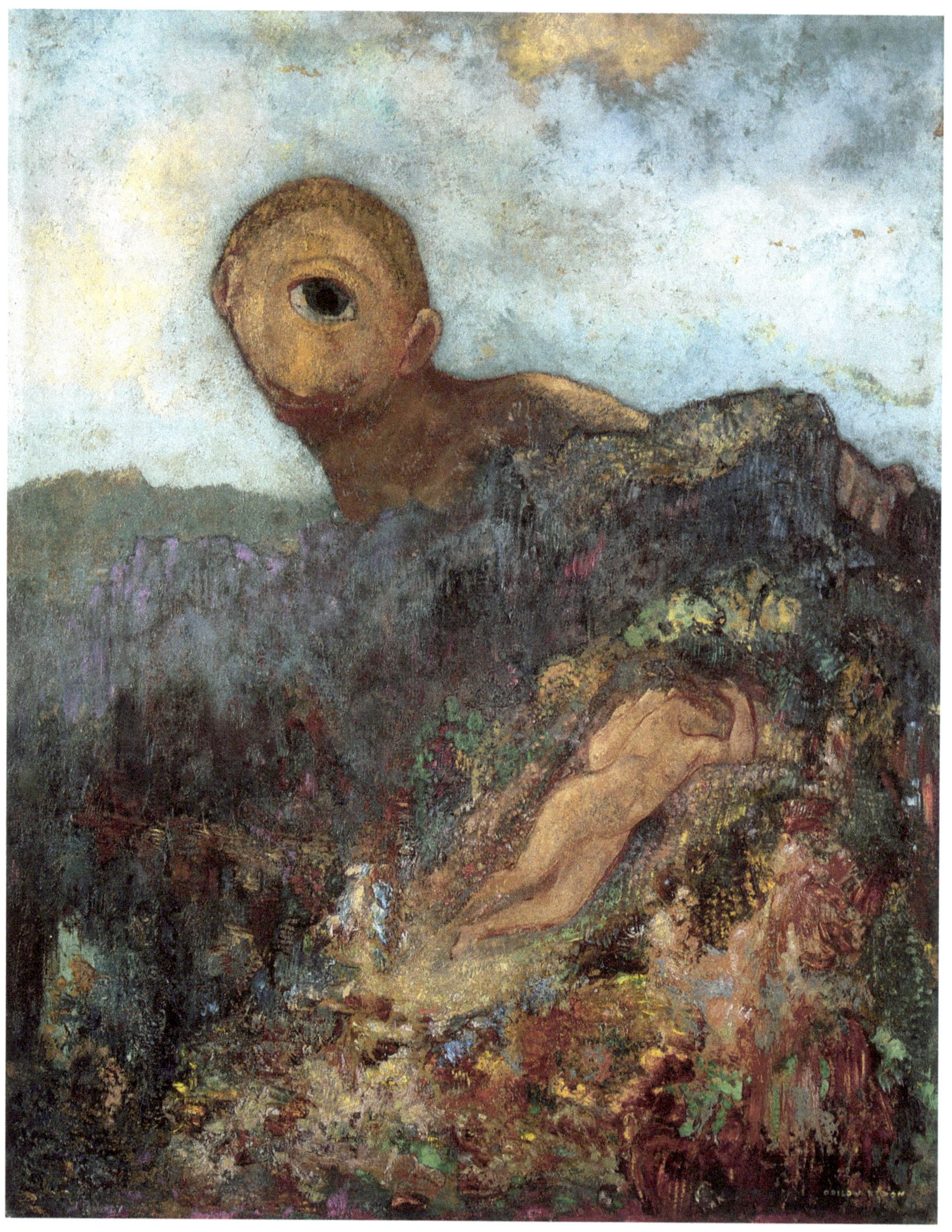

Odilon Redon

(Bordeaux, 1840 – Paris, 1916)

The son of a Creole mother and of a Frenchman who had set out to Louisiana to make his fortune, Bertrand-Jean Redon, called Odilon, was born on 20 April 1840, after his parents had returned to France and settled in Bordeaux. There, Redon would grow up and began to develop his feeling for art. Redon started drawing as a young child, and at the age of ten he was awarded a drawing prize at school. At the time of his first communion, Redon was moved by the powerful gothic architecture, but the brightly colored rays of light walled inside the place of worship by the old multi-colored stained glass windows affected him more than anything else.

Time spent in a milieu of simple country pleasures also stimulated Redon's identity as an artist. Lost among vast country spaces pervaded by the subtleties of nature, its contrasts of light and weather, Redon created his first drawings and charcoals at a very young age. But it was no doubt his journey to Paris and his visits to Parisian museums when he was but seven years old that persuaded Redon to choose a career as an artist. Returning to Bordeaux, the boy's destiny already seemed completely mapped out.

Attending day school and pursuing architectural studies hardly changed Redon's plans in the least, but contributed to the development of his skill at drawing and his lifelong attention to detail. From 1855 Redon took drawing classes under the tutelage of Stanislas Gorin, himself a student of Eugène Isabey d'Héroult, an independent art teacher and watercolor specialist. Gorin had a considerable effect on Redon's work, encouraging him to copy the canvases of Delacroix, and leading him to discover the art of Millet, Corot, and even Gustave Moreau.

In 1863 Redon met Rodolphe Bresdin, who introduced him to the art of printmaking and, in particular, the technique of etching. Redon proceeded to complete various albums and a large number of illustrations, primarily of Symbolist texts, including Baudelaire's *Fleurs du Mal*. After the war of 1870 Redon lived in Paris, but continued to visit the family estate, as well as Brittany.

In 1880 Redon married a young Creole woman named Camille Falte, and started making pastels. In 1884 he began to be well-known,

◀ **Odilon Redon,**
The Cyclops, c. 1898-1900.
Oil on wood, 64 x 51 cm.
Kröller-Müller Museum, Otterlo.

while his sombre subjects that had long focused on the theme of the prisoner and the depiction of oddities (such as creatures composed of insects with human heads) were discarded. His blacks were transformed into a flood of radiant colours that gave form to more personal ideas and emotions in which mythology meets the flowery landscapes of his dreams with unrivalled charm.

Odilon Redon died in Paris in 1916 at the age of seventy-six, leaving behind a considerable body of work as his legacy. The Nabis would claim ownership of this legacy and the Symbolists would draw on it as a source.

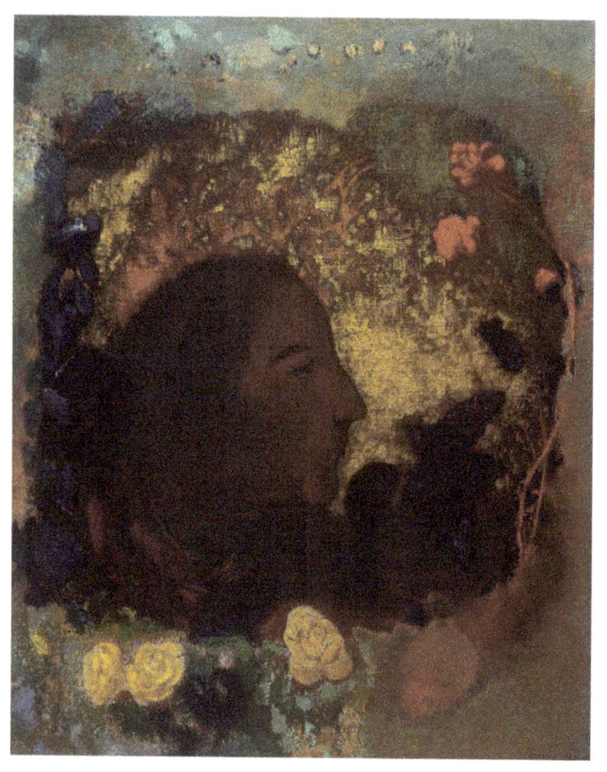

▲ **Odilon Redon**,
Paul Gauguin, 1903-1905.
Oil on canvas, 66 x 54.5 cm.
Musée d'Orsay, Paris.

due to his active participation in the "Salon des indépendants", coinciding with the publication of Joris-Karl Huysmans's novel *A Rebours (Against the Grain, also known as Against Nature)*, whose protagonist is a collector of Redon prints.

Over the years, and after conquering health problems, Redon saw his work evolving towards new colors simultaneously clear and bright,

Odilon Redon, ▶
Closed Eyes, 1890.
Oil on canvas remounted on board, 44 x 36 cm.
Musée d'Orsay, Paris.

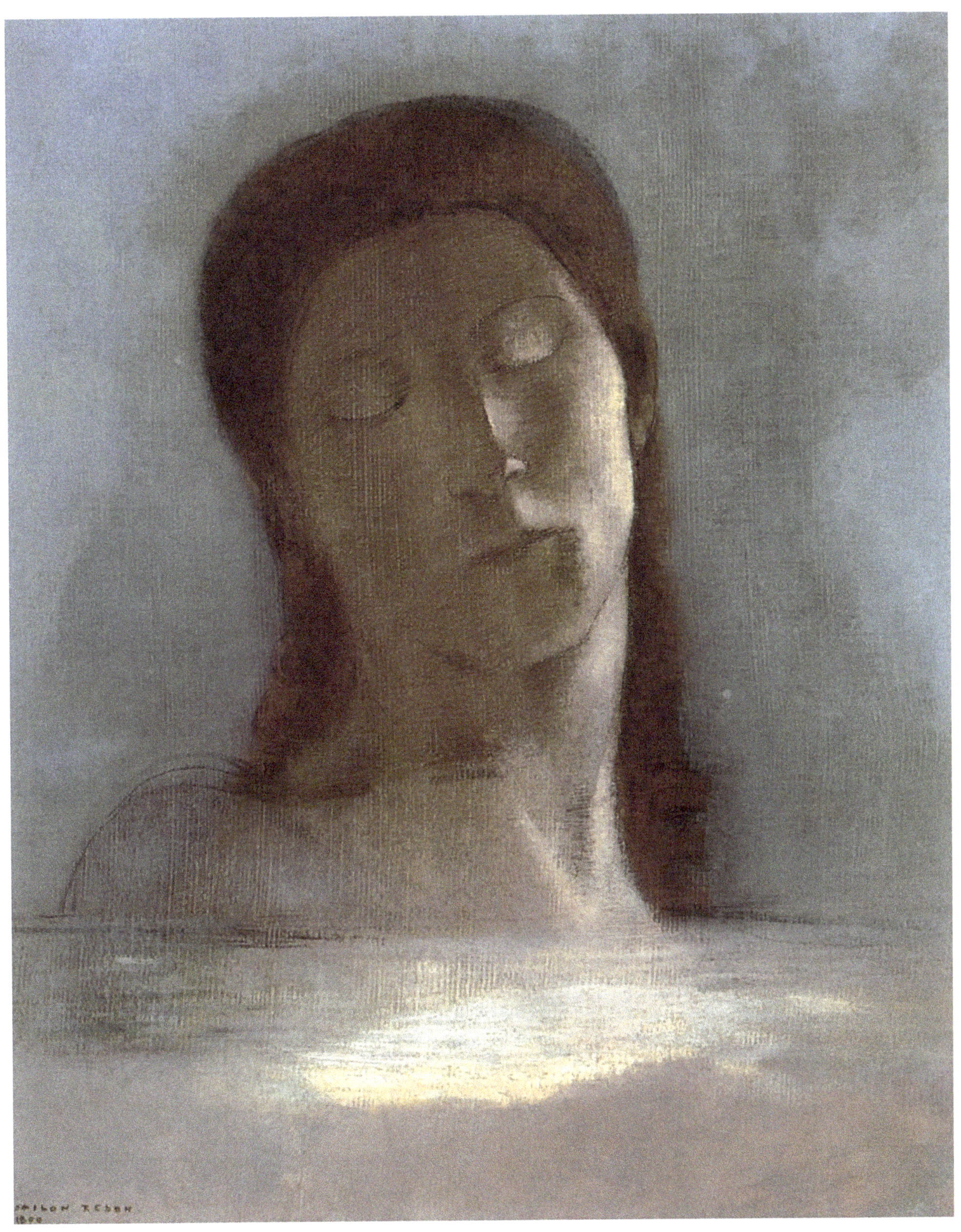

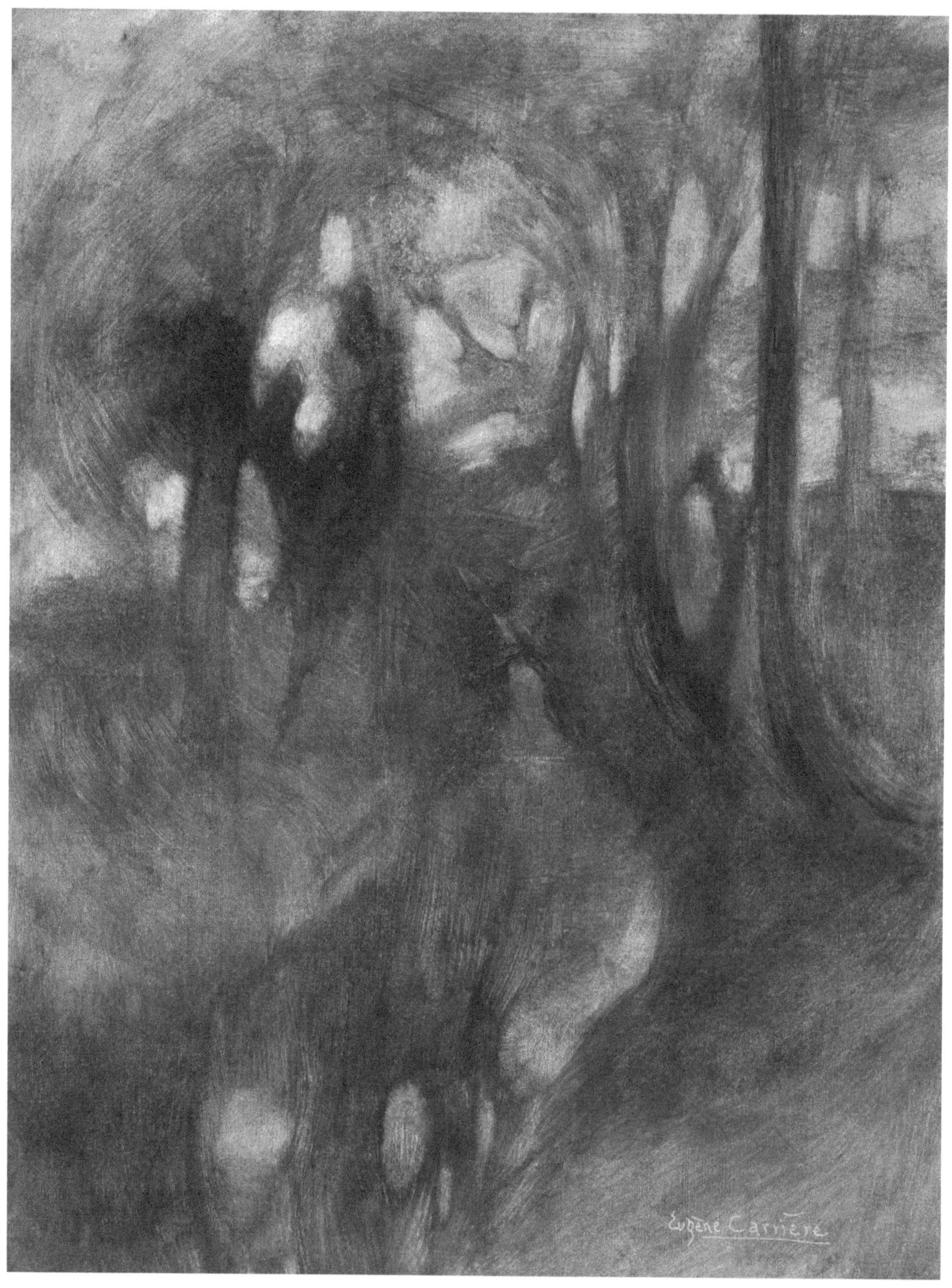

Eugène Carrière

Eugène Carrière

(Gournay-sur-Marne, 1849 – Paris, 1906)

Of Flemish and Alsatian parentage, Eugène Carrière was born in Gournay-sur-Marne on 16 January 1849. Carrière left the Paris region and grew up in Strasbourg, but would return to Paris to enrol in the "Ecole des Beaux-Arts" (against the advice of his father) in 1869. Although his childhood was more marked by nature walks and memories of the outdoors than by works of art, Carrière began at a very young age to commit to paper all the visible forms he was inexplicably interested in. He attended the design school in Strasbourg from the age of thirteen, entering a lithography studio in 1864.

In Paris Carrière frequented the studio of the academic painter Alexandre Cabanel, then attended the "Ecole des Beaux-Arts" from 1873. Three years later he endured a failed attempt to win the Prix de Rome, but participated in his first Salon.

Inspired in particular by Dutch painting, Carrière painted a number of important family interiors, including several relating to motherhood. Carrière's style began to evolve in the 1880s, and he started to free himself from the academic influences stemming from his previously received education.

In 1890 he participated in the Salon of the "Société nationale des Beaux-Arts" and took up lithography again. It was no doubt at this time that Carrière produced a truly personal style. From then on his works were characterised by monochrome, stylised detail, and sometimes distorted elements. By employing a carefully chosen tonality, he extracted portraits, intimate scenes, and other landscapes out of evanescent forms. Standing before these works, the viewer encounters true paradoxes where suffering responds to love; gentleness conquers violence; and man and devil come face to face with woman and angel. True distillations of meaning, sources of light in deep darkness, all the forms re-interpreted in Carrière's work represent the essence of life, forcing the viewer to question what he might have previously considered paradoxical.

A passionate humanist, concerned in particular with education issues, completely anchored in the era in which he lived, Carrière participated in the debates of his time, in particular during the Dreyfus Affair (when he committed himself to Zola) and on the subject of the emancipation

◀ **Eugène Carrière,**
Meditation II. Portrait of a Girl.
Private collection.

of women. Always more interested in what united people, as opposed to what separated them, the refinement of his work often seemed to the reflect the man that he was.

In 1898 he opened an "academy" which would train Derain and Matisse, among others. Carrière's contemporaries paid him a sincere tribute in 1904 when Auguste Rodin organised a banquet in his honor. Throughout his career, his painting, far from restricting itself to portraits and interior scenes, embraced most pictorial genres, always in response to Symbolist concerns. Suffering from throat cancer, Carrière underwent surgery that left him paralysed and unable to talk during the last year of his life. But he was a man who was well liked by many, and his friends continued to pay him visits, engaging in written conversations with him. Carrière died in Paris on 27 March 1906.

The Musée d'Orsay celebrated the centenary of his death with the Rodin-Eugène Carrière exhibition and also through the publication of the "catalogue raisonné" of his painted works, a final homage.

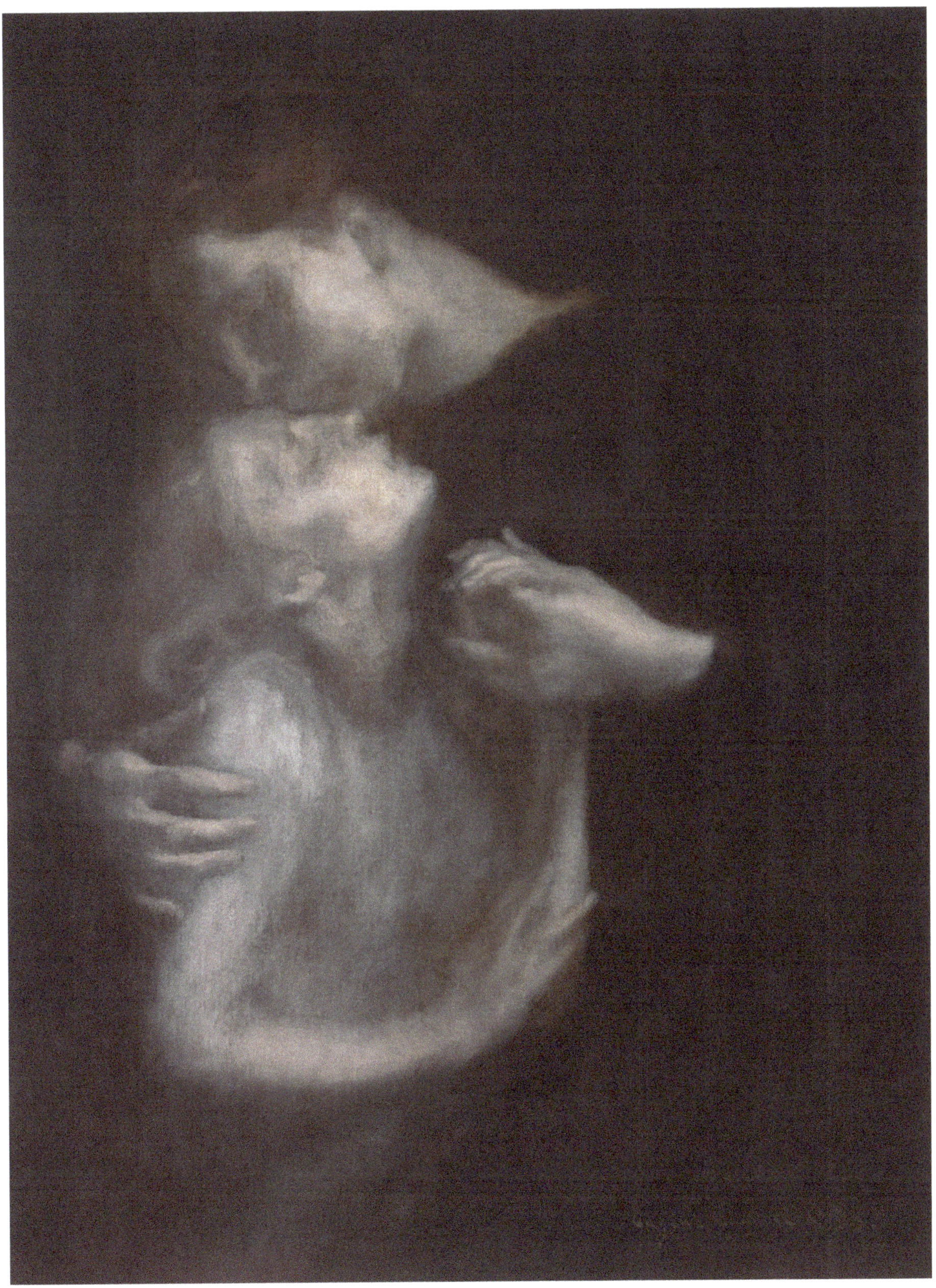

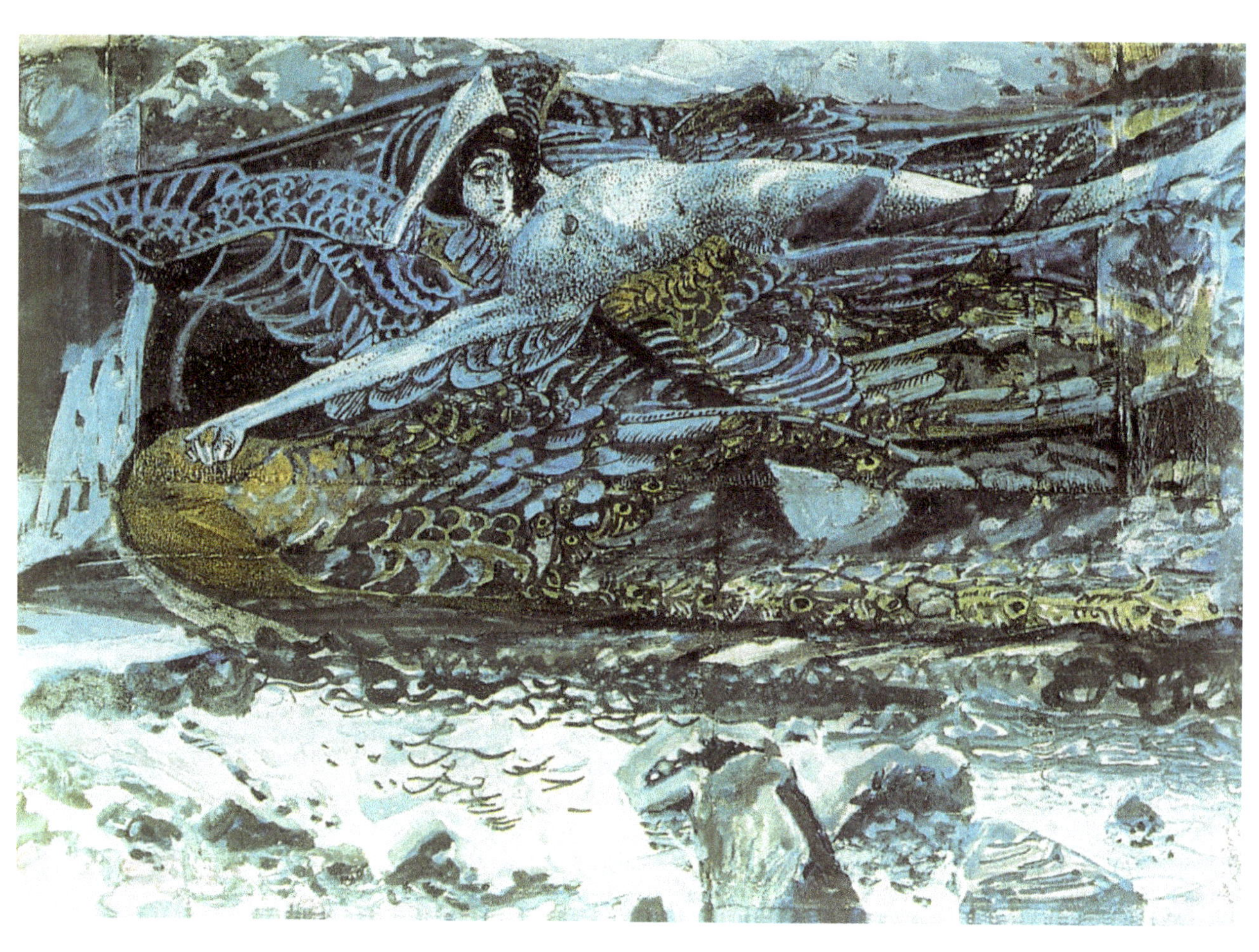

▲ **Mikhail Aleksandrovich Vrubel**,*Quick-Tempered Demon,* 1901.
Watercolour, gouache, and colours on paper, 21 x 30 cm.
Sketch for the painting of 1902. The Pushkin Museum of Fine Arts, Moscow.

Mikhail Aleksandrovich Vrubel

(Omsk, 1856 – St Petersburg, 1910)

The son of a Russian army colonel, Mikhail Aleksandrovich Vrubel was born in the town of Omsk in Siberia. Encouraged by his father, Vrubel commenced a thorough study of history, music, theatre, and literature, as well as languages (Latin, German and French). His actual artistic training began in 1864, when he entered the Society for the Encouragement of the Arts in Saint Petersburg. Between 1874 and 1880, Vrubel studied law, and then attended classes at the Academy of Arts in Saint Petersburg. There, alongside Valentin Serov, he studied under the painter and graphic artist Pavel Tchistiakov, who would play an important role in the development of his style.

In 1884 Vrubel's professors recommended that he be given the job of restoring the icons and ancient frescos of a church in Kiev. This experience led Vrubel to think about how spirituality and expressions could be depicted and how to approach issues relating to monumentality. At the same time he was doing decorations for the theatre, opera, and even private properties. He was also involved in ceramic work and developed a method of firing that enabled him to give his works a metallic sheen. Vrubel's style continued to evolve up until the 1890s, when he moved to Moscow. In compositions always marked by considerable Symbolism, he made his forms geometric (by cutting and crossing lines) and employed colours with exceptional emotional sensitivity. As a result, his canvases often recall glasswork. It was in this period that Vrubel began a series of canvases on the theme of *The Demon*, inspired by a poem by Mikhail Lermontov. At the same time, Vrubel joined the Abramtsevo colony, an elitist circle that was the cradle of Russian painting and culture during the late nineteenth century.

Unfortunately Vrubel suffered from mental problems during the last ten years of his life. After a stay in a clinic, his health returned, only to decline again a few years later. He was consequently forced to commit himself to an asylum on several occasions, but continued to paint in spite of his health problems. Between 1902 and 1905 he devoted himself primarily to drawing, completing in particular beautiful compositions in black and white. But with his mental health always on the decline, Vrubel was unable to finish the portrait of the poet Valeri Brioussov that he was working on in 1906. In the spring of 1910, while deeply depressed, Vrubel sat before an open window hoping that he might catch a cold bad enough to release him from his demons. The artist died of pneumonia in April 1910.

In 2006, as part of the *Europalia Russie* festival, the community museum of Ixelles in Belgium staged an exhibition devoted to Russian Symbolism within which Vrubel occupied a major position. By being the leading Russian Symbolist, as well as a practitioner of the decorative arts, he was able to re-interpret Russia's plastic arts. A unique character, Vrubel remains a profoundly original and independent artist who led Russian art to the threshold of the twentieth century, he alone making the transition between the old and new generation of Russian artists.

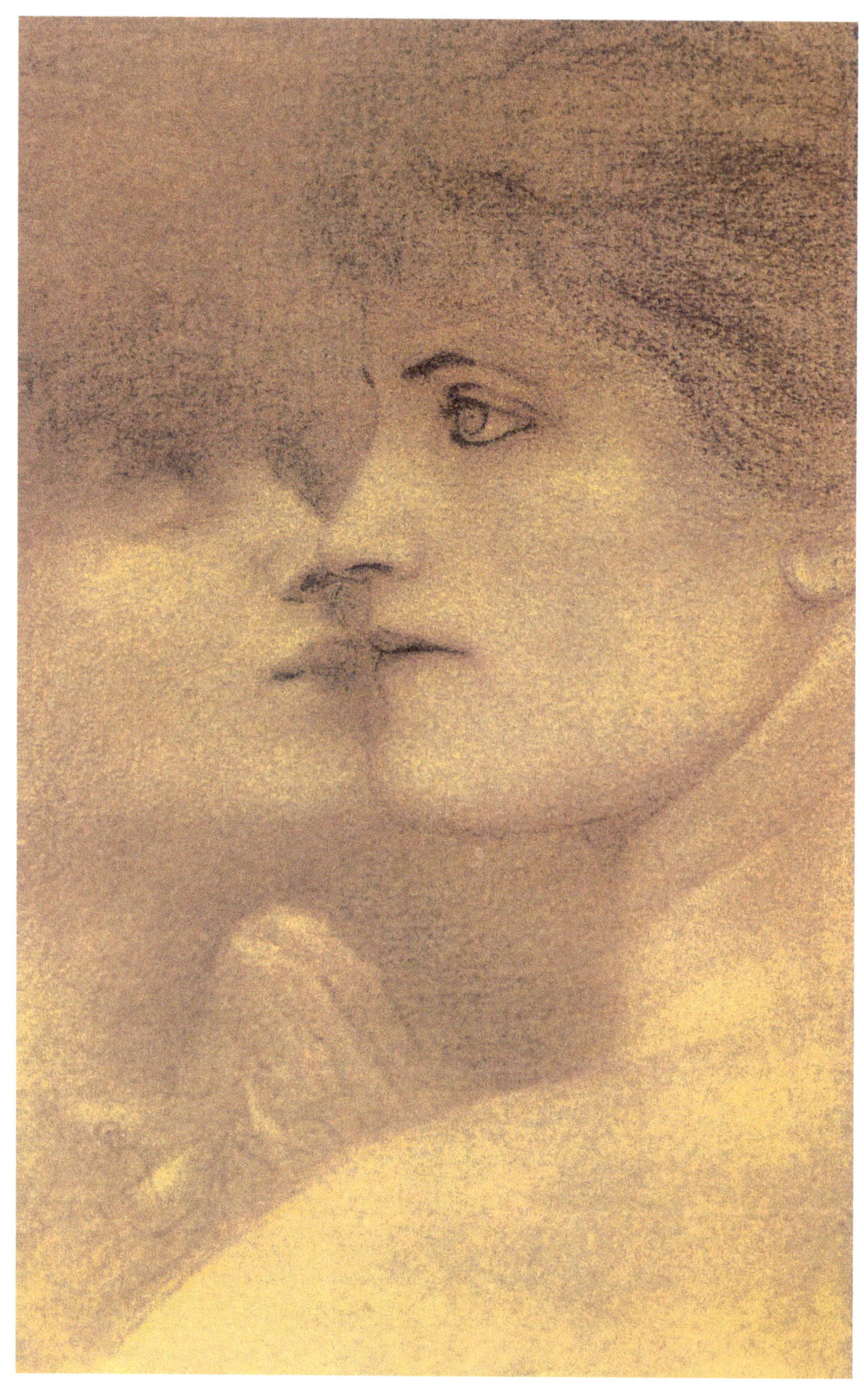

▲ **Fernand Khnopff**, *Study of Women*, c. 1887.
Red chalk on paper, 12.5 x 8.5 cm. Private collection, New York

Fernand Khnopff

(Grembergen-les-Termonde, 1858 – Brussels, 1921)

The son of a magistrate, Fernand Edmond Jean-Marie Khnopff was born in Grembergen-lez-Termonde, Belgium, in 1858. He was the eldest of three children. In 1859 his father was appointed a public prosecutor, and the Khnopff family moved to Bruges. His brother Georges, a future musician, poet, and art critic, was born in 1860; his sister Marguerite was born in 1864. The year after her birth the Khnopff family moved again to go and live in Brussels.

In the Belgian capital Khnopff continued his education by studying at the Faculty of Law at the Université Libre, and began frequenting Xavier Mellery's painting studio. Sometime between 1876 and 1879 he interrupted his law studies in order to enter the Brussels l'Académie des beaux-arts, where he met James Ensor. Khnopff's first paintings were mainly landscapes, depicting in particular the town of Fosset where he normally summered.

Inspired by the writing of Gustave Flaubert, Khnopff painted his first Symbolist work in 1883 and participated in the founding of *Les Vingt*. Mentioned in the influential art magazine *L'Art Moderne*, Khnopff appeared in the annual exhibitions of "Les Vingt" until the group disbanded ten years later.

In 1885, while fascinated by the occult theories of the Rosicrucians, Khnopff met Joséphin Péladan, for whose novels he illustrated the frontispieces. Khnopff

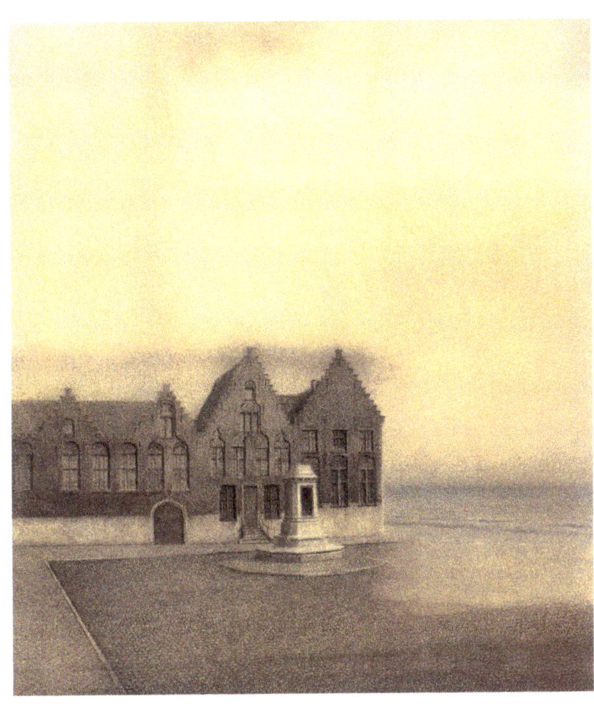

▲ **Fernand Khnopff**,
A Deserted Town, 1904.
Charcoal drawing with black pencil and pastel on paper
mounted on canvas, 76 x 69 cm.
Musées royaux des Beaux-Arts de Belgique, Brussels.

regularly exhibited in the Salon of the Rosicrucians. In 1887 Khnopff completed the enigmatic portrait of his younger sister, Marguerite, which he thereafter always kept with him. As a woman who was both pure and sexually attractive, in the eyes of the painter she represented a type of feminine ideal, and it was she whom Khnopff depicted several times in his masterpiece *Memories*, painted in the subsequent year.

Particularly active in the bourgeois milieus of Brussels and Paris, Khnopff quickly became the portraitist of choice. In 1889 Khnopff, who was drawn to England, began to develop relationships with Pre-Raphaelite painters, especially Burne-Jones. The following year, the Hanover Gallery in London held an exhibition devoted to Khnopff. During this period he participated in many international exhibitions in London, Munich, Venice, and Paris.

Khnopff is known for the faded tonalities of his colours that increase the viewer's experience of nostalgia and detachment when viewing his paintings. While a correspondent for Belgium, he was also associated with the art magazine *The Studio*, for which he worked until 1914. In June 1898 the Austrian Secession (an Art Nouveau offshoot), welcomed Khnopff as a guest of honour, alongside Rodin and Puvis de Chavannes. Khnopff composed his famous canvas *Les Caresses (Caresses)* the same year.

In 1903 the financier Adolphe Stoclet commissioned Khnopff to decorate the music room of his Art Nouveau mansion, the Palais Stoclet, which also included Gustav Klimt's famous mosaic murals. At the same time, Khnopff started a series of pastels around Georges Rodenbach's Symbolist novel *Bruges la Morte (The Dead City of Bruges)* and designed costumes for various operas playing at the Théâtre de la Monnaie in Brussels.

In 1908 he married Marthe Worms, but the marriage lasted only three years. Fernand Khnopff died in Brussels on November 12, 1921 and the work of the "painter of closed eyes" then became an essential representative of the Symbolist movement

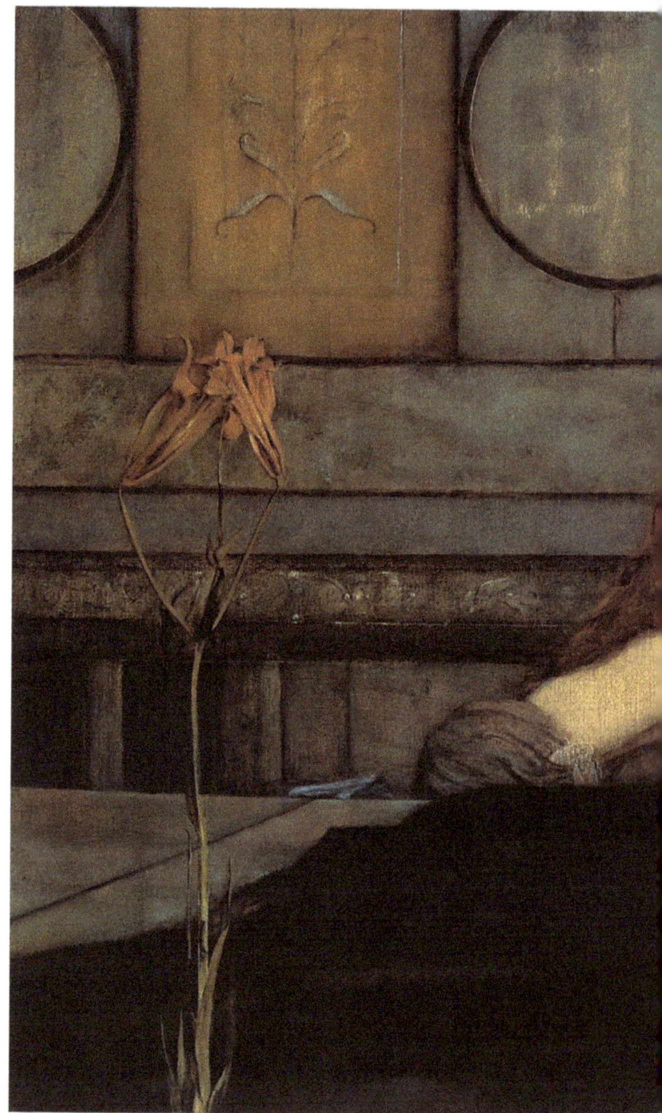

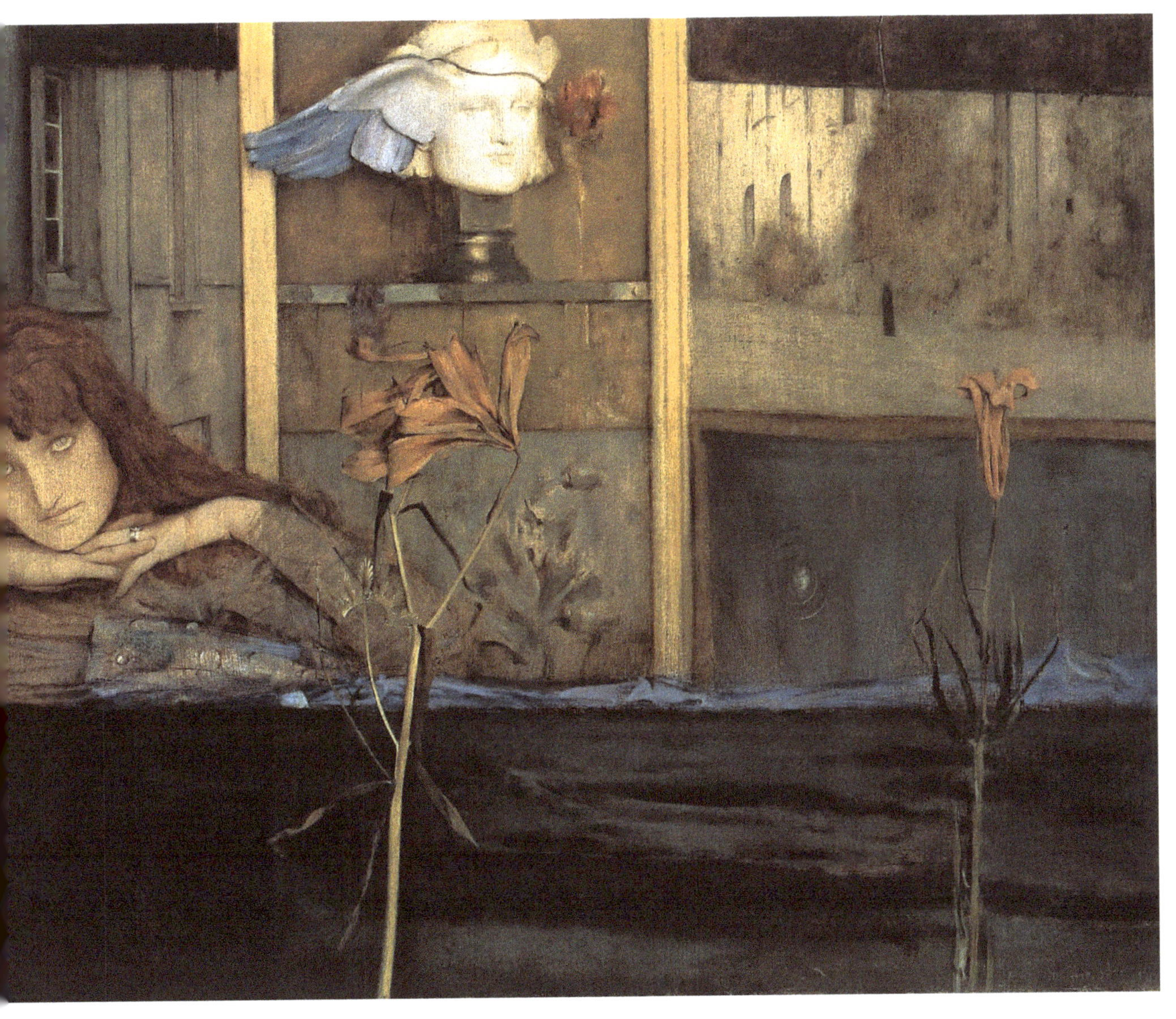

▲ **Fernand Khnopff**,
I Lock My Door Upon Myself, 1891.
Oil on canvas, 72.7 x 141 cm.
Neue Pinakothek, Munich..

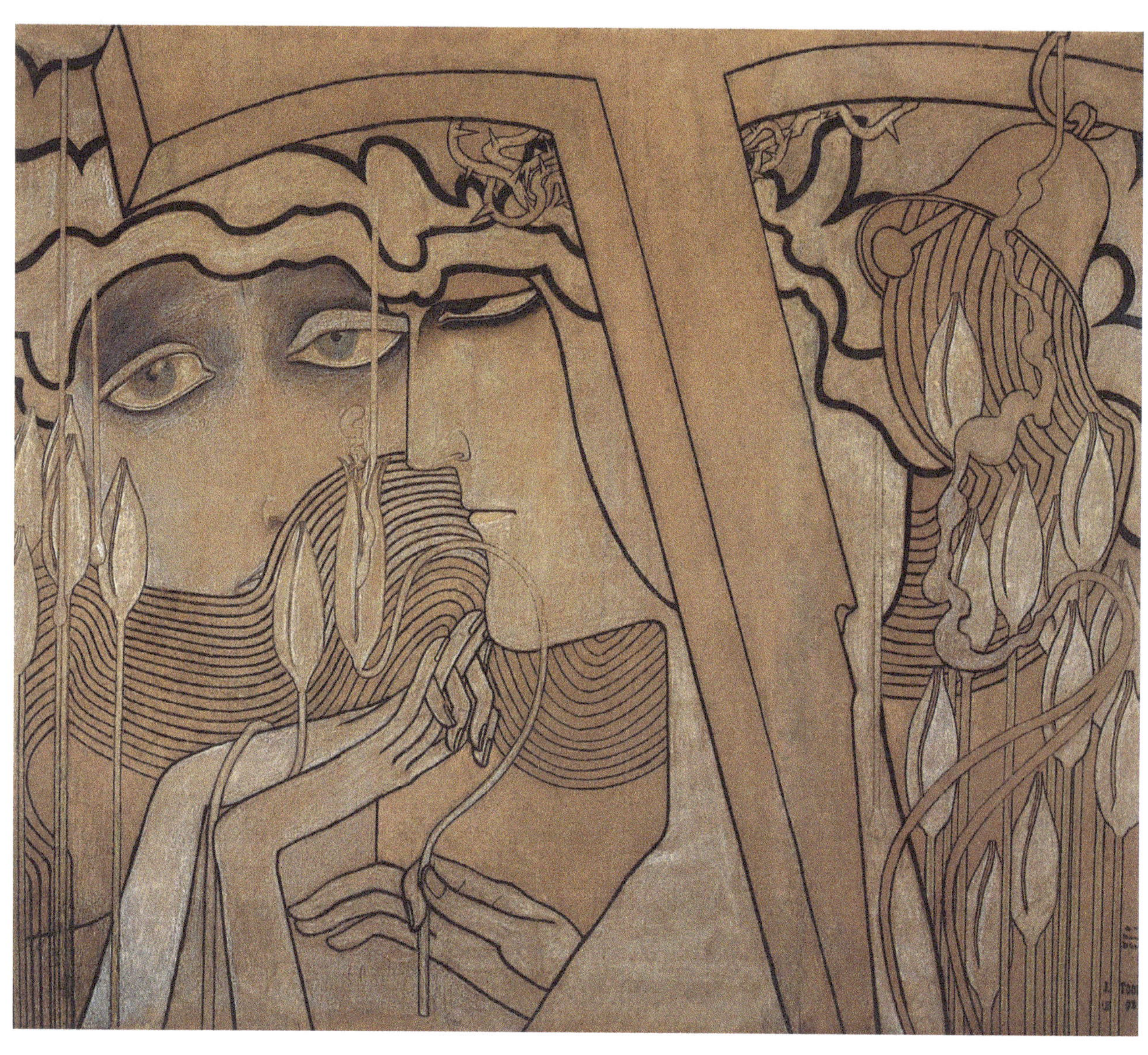

▲ **Jan Toorop**, *Desire and Satisfaction*, 1893.
Pastel, 76 x 90 cm. Musée d'Orsay, Paris.

Jan Toorop

(Purworedjo, 1858 – The Hague, 1928)

The son of a civil servant, whose job required travel to Dutch trading posts, and an English mother, Johannes Théodor Toorop, known as Jan Toorop, was born on the island of Java in Indonesia in 1858. In 1863 the Toorop family moved to the island of Banka in southern Sumatra. Upon returning to the Netherlands in 1869, Jan Toorop attended secondary schools in Leiden and Winterswijk. In 1881 he continued his education at the Academy of Amsterdam in the town of Delft.

As a result of his background, Toorop developed a highly individual style in which he combined Javanese motifs with Symbolist influences. In 1882 he moved to Brussels where he enrolled in the Academy of Decorative Arts. Two years later he exhibited in Paris in the "Salon des Artistes indépendants" and in Brussels joined "Les Vingt". Toorop also made several trips to England, where he discovered the works of the Pre-Raphaelites.

In 1886 he married Annie Hall and three years later they settled in England, where Toorop prepared an exhibition showcasing the *Les Vingt* artists for display in Amsterdam. A year later he returned to the Netherlands and began painting his first pointillist canvases inspired by Seurat.

Around 1890 Toorop encountered Symbolism when he discovered Belgian writer Maurice Maeterlinck's poetry, which Toorop considered a revelation. His art would henceforth appear Symbolist, primarily on account of his frequent use of mythological subjects. Additionally, the scrolls and curls of Toorop's paintings, evoking shadow puppet theatre, are like the designs of decorative Art Nouveau wallpaper. In depictions of all sorts of genuine mysteries, Toorop based his figures on a feminine silhouette with long, willowy arms interlaced with infinite waves of long hair, and placed them in a world where heaven and earth had no boundaries.

During this period the artist also designed several posters and illustrated various works. In 1905 Toorop entered upon the path of religion and saw in it a second revelation. Baptised as a Protestant at the age of ten, he converted to Catholicism and henceforth structured his work around his faith. His art thus became more religious and mystical. Toorop subsequently refined his lines and simplified his style. He died in The Hague in 1928.

Until the twentieth-century rupture, Toorop's art filled the gap between Symbolism and Art Nouveau in a remarkable manner. His departures make him one of the most brilliant representatives of these movements, whereas the different developments of his style make him a precursor of most of the avant-garde movements of the twentieth century.

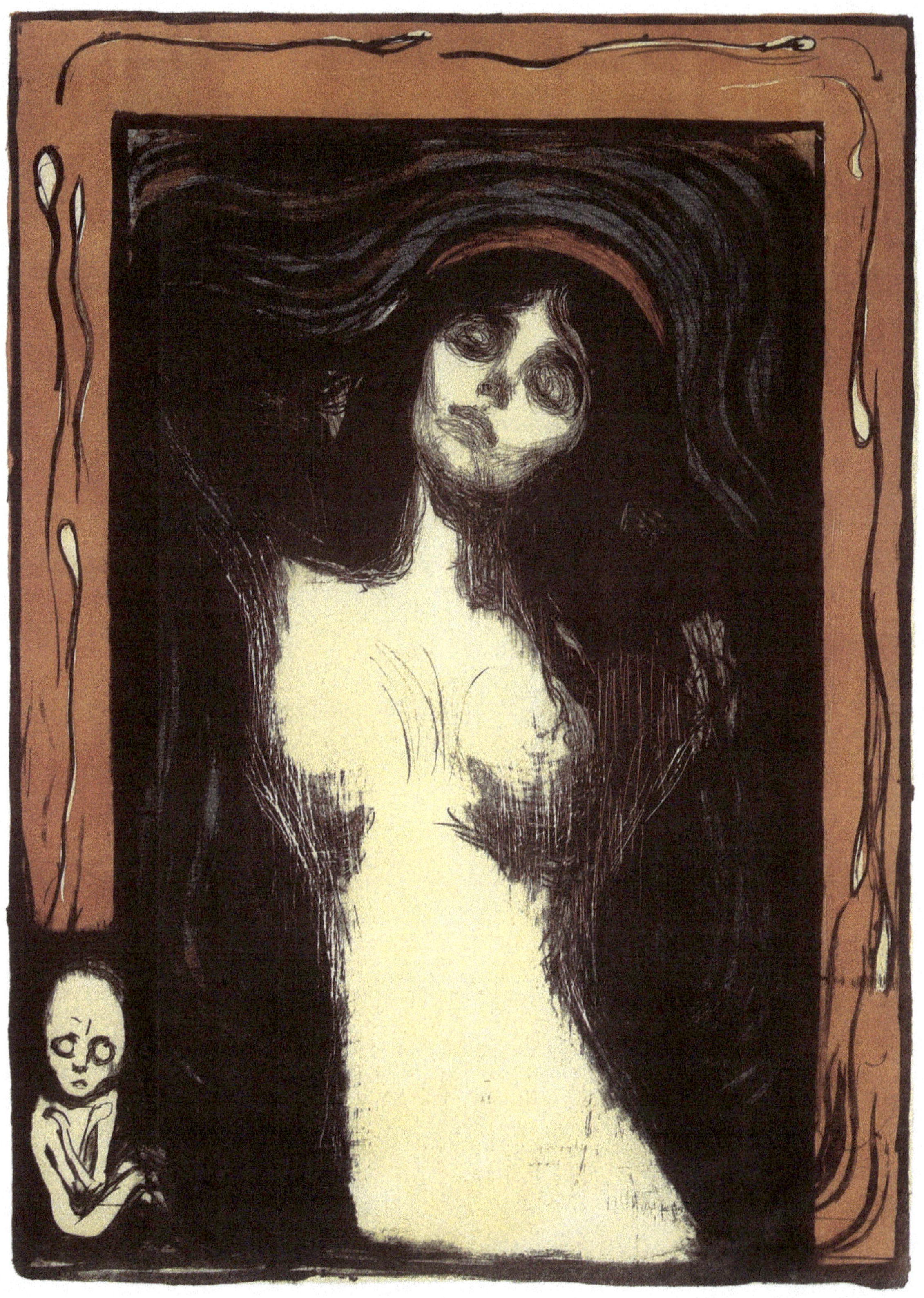

Edvard Munch

(Løten, 1863 – Ekely, 1944)

Throughout his career, the work of Edvard Munch would be affected by his childhood tragedies: the death of his mother when he was five and the death of his sister when she was just fifteen. Born in Løten in 1863, Munch grew up in the Norwegian capital of Christiana, now known as Oslo. In 1881 he enrolled in the Royal College of Art and Design under the direction of the sculptor Julius Middelthum, where he only gradually turned to painting, the medium that would truly showcase his talent.

The following year Munch studied with the naturalistic painters Christian Krohg and Frits Thaulow. As a result of his apprenticeship with these masters, his first canvases from the 1880s, such as *Landscape, Maridalem (outside Oslo)*, and even *The Old Church of Aker*, are in a particularly naturalistic vein. Munch nevertheless quickly cast off these influences, and, as he was a particularly gifted student, became Norway's prodigy. In 1883 he began to participate in exhibitions and was then included in the Salon of Decorative Arts and a group exhibition in Christiana. Munch's

◀ **Edvard Munch,**
Madonna, 1895-1902.
Lithograph, 60.5 x 44.5 cm.
The Museum of Modern Art, New York.

canvases, however, were still naturalistic and did not attract much attention.

In 1885 Munch started composing *The Sick Child,* an outlet for the guilt he felt over his sister's death, and then participated in the Universal Exposition in Anvers. The same year he travelled to France for the first time, visiting the Salon and the Louvre in Paris. Returning to Norway, Munch participated in Christiana's Autumn Exposition, where he publicly exhibited *The Sick Child,* which caused a scandal.

During the last decade of the nineteenth century, he had his first one-man exhibition at the Christiana Students' Association, and a student prize enabled him to return to Paris. Munch's canvases were henceforth marked by the profound torments that haunted the painter's soul and gave birth to Expressionism.

Often symbolic, Munch's works became true indications of his emotions and feelings. In 1892 he was invited to participate in an exhibition of the Berlin Artists' Union, but his works caused a serious scandal and the exhibition space that was devoted to Munch was closed after one week. The next year he started working on *The Frieze of Life,* a series of four canvases (*The Voice, The Scream, Anxiety,* and *The Ashes*) and made several

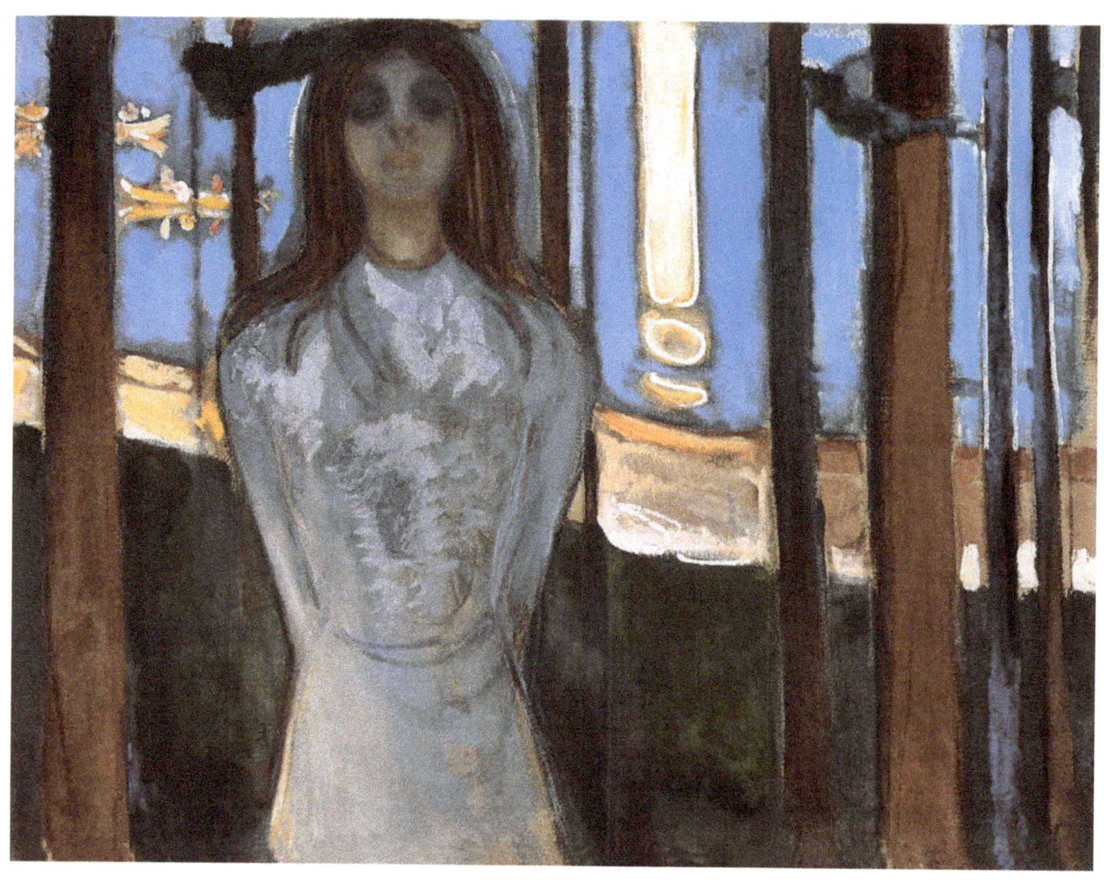

lithographs. During the last years of the century, Munch also met numerous artists and authors, in particular Symbolists and the Nabis, with whom he associated on Mallarmé's Tuesdays.

Despite health problems and the wounds of stormy love affairs, Munch entered a productive period at the dawn of the twentieth century and experienced significant success, in particular at the Exposition of Prague in 1905. Surviving

an outbreak of Spanish influenza in 1919, he had a retrospective at the national galleries of Berlin and Oslo in 1927 that featured 223 of his works. Ten years later, however, Munch's work was seized from German museums after the Nazis labelled it "degenerate art." During the German occupation of Norway, Munch led a solitary life of seclusion. He died on 23 January 1944, leaving his complete *oeuvre* to the city of Oslo.

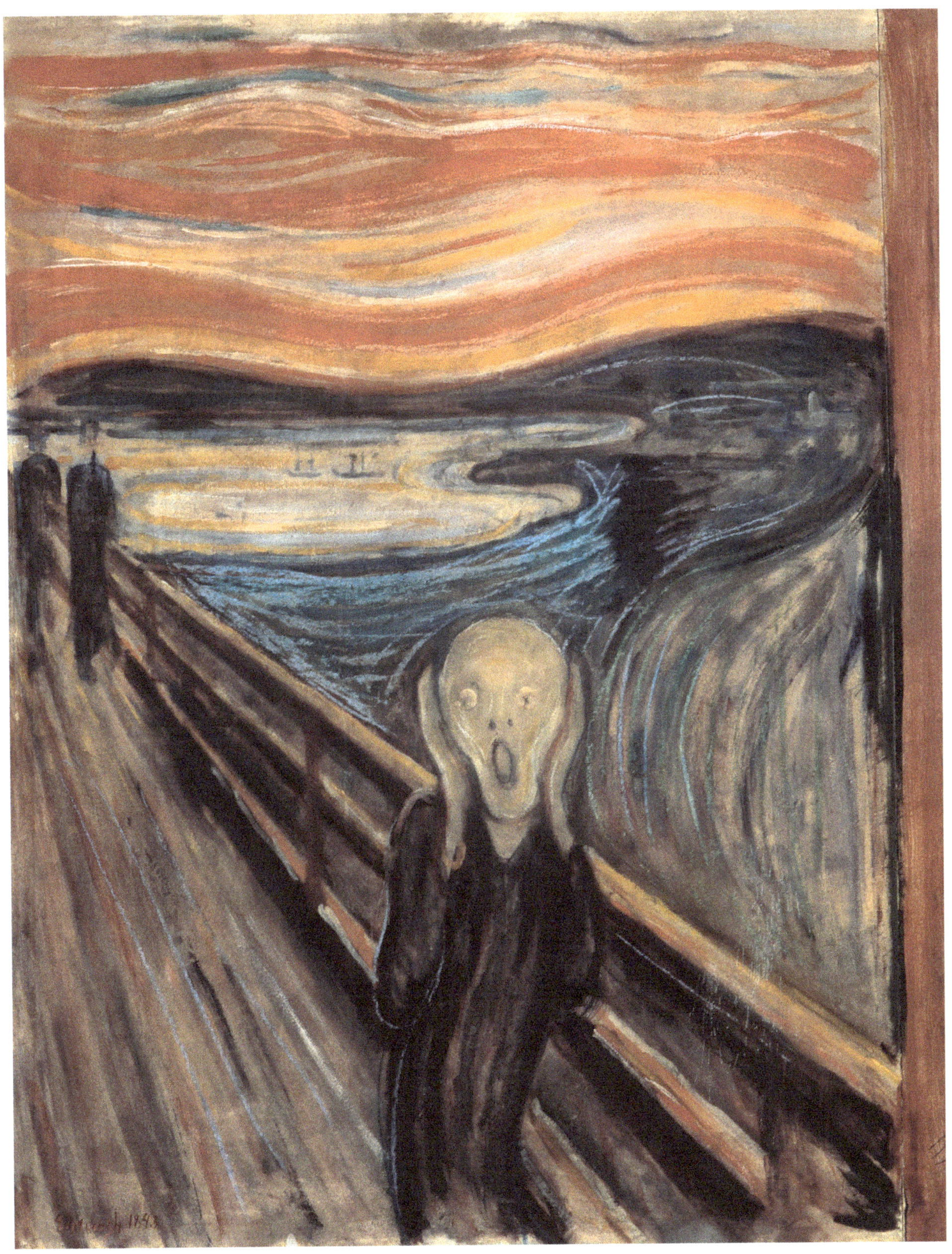

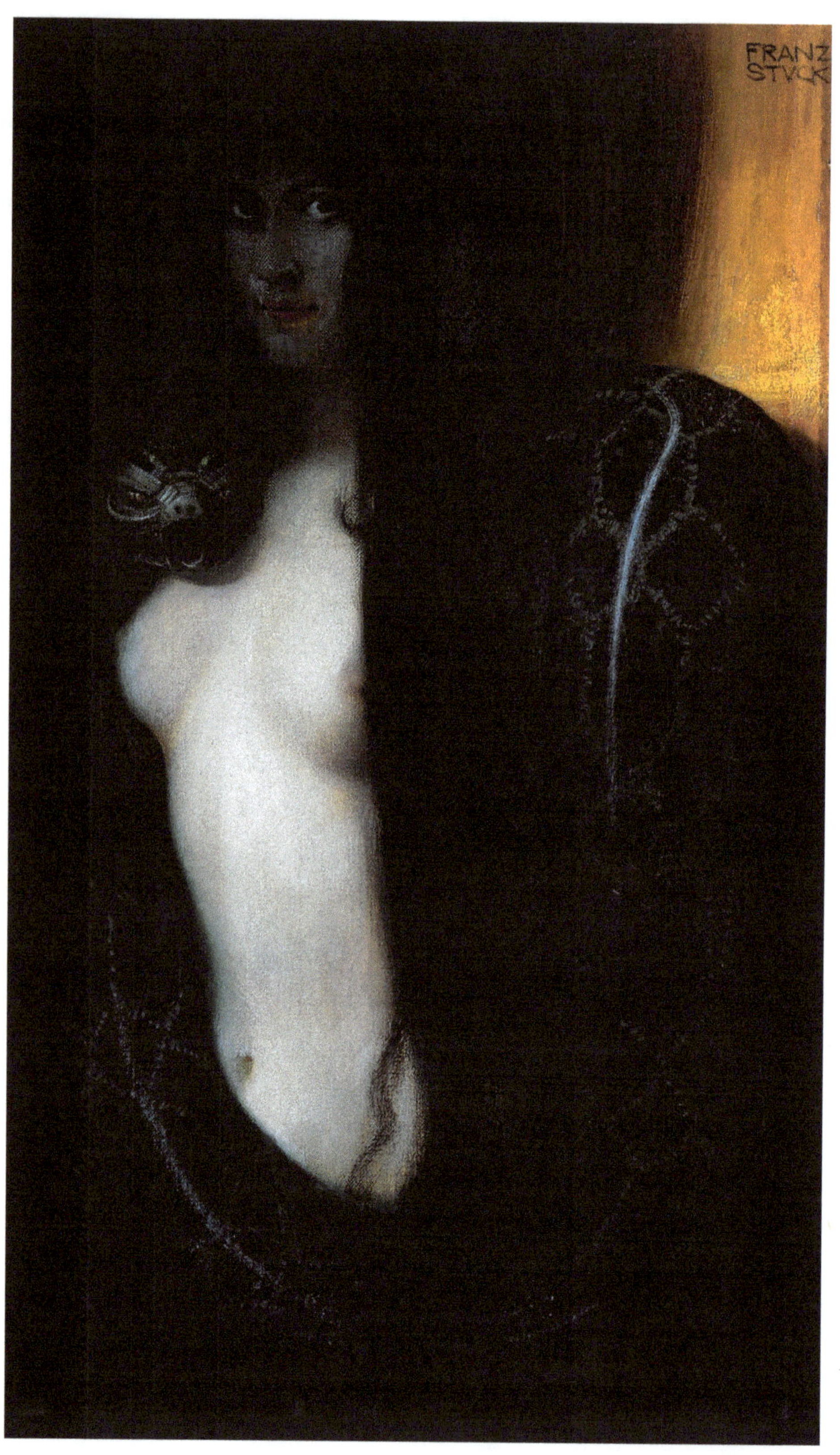

FRANZ
STVCK

Franz von Stuck

(Tettenweis, 1863 – Munich, 1928)

Franz von Stuck was born in the Bavarian town of Tettenweis in 1863. From 1878 to 1881 he attended the *Kunstgewerbeschule* in Munich, where he was encouraged by the painter Ferdinand Barth, then continued his artistic training at the Academy of Munich, where he met Wilhelm Lindenschmit and Ferdinand Löfftz, until 1885.

But von Stuck did not devote himself entirely to painting until 1889. A versatile artist with diverse interests, he also made decorative paintings and worked on publishing the humorist magazine *Fliegende Blätter*, as well as the series *Allegorien und Embleme* and *Karten und Vignetten*, which he illustrated. These activities were vital in establishing his reputation as a skilled draughtsman with a good sense of humour.

At the same time, von Stuck obtained a perfect union of masterful drawing and intensity of colour in his paintings. If he tackled mythological and allegorical subjects, the symbolic treatment he gave them caused all conventionality to be forgotten. In 1889 he received a Gold Medal at the annual *Künstlergenossenschaft* exhibition, where he showed *The Guardian of Paradise*. Despite this acknowledgment, von Stuck nevertheless remained widely criticised by curators who called his work 'daub'. But in 1893, at the exhibition of the Munich Secession, a group in which he played an active role, his glorification of *The Sin* was a success and caused a sensation. In this depiction of Eve wrapped in a serpent, von Stuck created not only one of his now most widely-known paintings, but also a work emblematic of the Symbolist movement.

Von Stuck died in Munich in August 1928. Considered one of the most popular and widely known artists in Europe at the turn of the century, his work was called into question by artists, critics, and the public after his death. He had to wait until the period 1960-70 and the revival of interest in late-nineteenth century aesthetic movements for his vast and varied Œuvre to be re-evaluated and re-established in its proper place.

◀ **Franz von Stuck**,
The Sin, 1893.
Oil on canvas, 94.5 x 59.5 cm.
Neue Pinakothek, Munich.

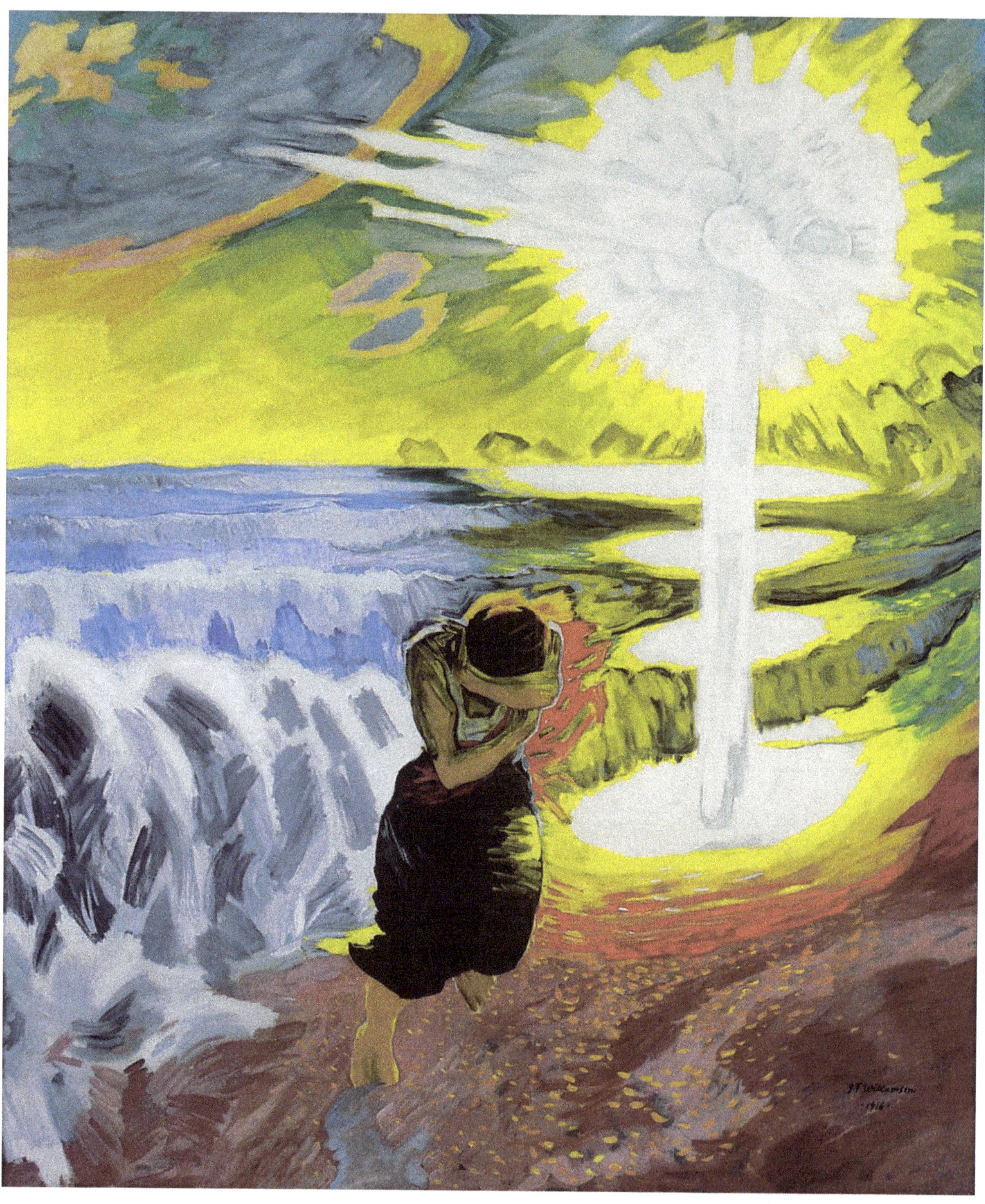

Jens Ferdinand Willumsen

(Copenhagen, 1863 – Le Canet, 1958)

Born in Copenhagen in 1863 of English parentage, Jens Ferdinand Willumsen entered the Royal Academy of Fine Arts of that city in 1881. Willumsen was taking architecture classes at the same time and later sharpened his technique under the painter Peder Severin Kroyer.

In 1888 he made his first trip to France. Upon his arrival, he thoroughly immersed himself in the culture of *fin de siècle* Paris. His initial canvases were in a naturalistic style. In 1890 he met Paul Sérusier and Maurice Denis and discovered the work of the Symbolist Odilon Redon through Theo Van Gogh. During a summer trip to Brittany in that same year he met Gauguin and visited him at Pont-Aven and Le Pouldu. Steeping himself in the works of these major artists, Willumsen also borrowed from the German Expressionist groups, the Danish school, and Nordic Symbolism.

Already recognised in France, Willumsen's fame also grew after the 1900 Universal Exposition held in Paris, where he exhibited *Jotunheim*. It is a work of masterful geometricised Symbolism, in which sculpture combines perfectly with painting, particularly in the intensity of the canvas and its frame. Painted between 1892 and 1893, after a stay in Norway, the work was very popular with the public.

After this period Willumsen, a great traveller, never stopped pushing himself beyond boundaries. He visited the United States, Italy, Spain (where he discovered and admired El Greco), and North Africa, returning to live in France in 1916. Although only rarely going back to Denmark, he exhibited there regularly.

Painting remained Willumsen's preferred means of expression, but he nevertheless explored different visual art forms throughout his career. Working in this way he developed multiple talents, practising painting at the same time as engraving, photography, and ceramics. His output therefore was related to the use of many different techniques. Additionally, his style was always changing and following the various aesthetic trends of the period. Willumsen adapted his themes, which became simultaneously naturalist, symbolic, and expressionist. But his *oeuvre* will always be characterised by the use of lively colour and theatrical effects that bear witness to his singular and original personality, always in search of freedom.

Jens Ferdinand Willumsen died at Canet in 1958 at the age of eighty-five.

◀ **Jens Ferdinand Willumsen,**
Fear of Nature. After the Storm, No. 2., 1916.
Oil on canvas, 194 x 169 cm.
J. F. Willumsens Museum, Frederikssund.

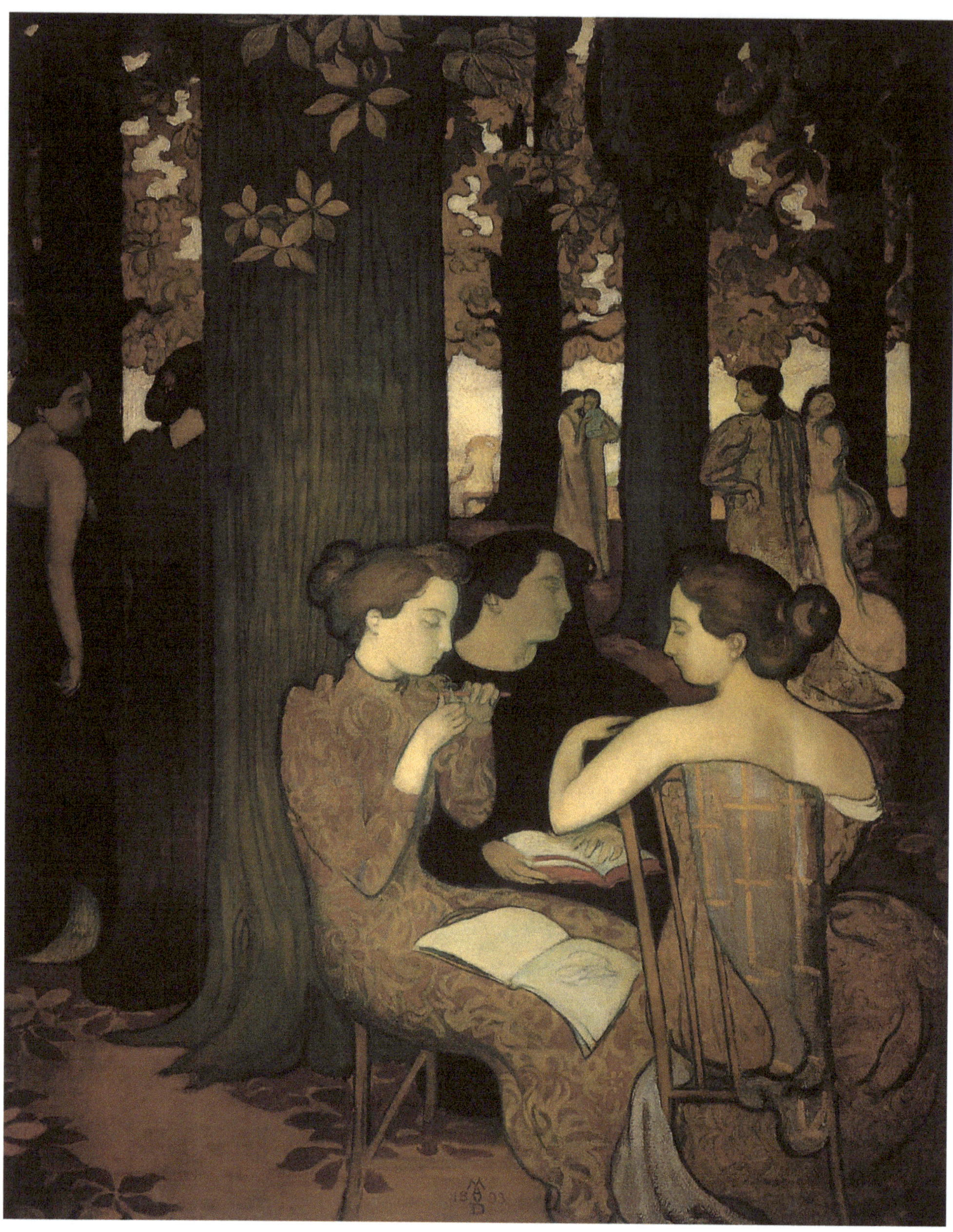

Maurice Denis

(Granville, 1870 – Paris, 1943)

Born in Granville, while his father, a French railway employee, was away on business, Maurice Denis would live his entire life in Saint-Germain-en-Laye.At the age of twelve he got off to a brilliant start in his education at the Lycée Condorcet, a secondary school in Paris where Edouard Vuillard and Ker-Xavier Roussel (1867 – 1944) were also registered. In 1888 Denis was attending the Ecole Nationale des Beaux-Arts and the Académie Julian at the same time.

At the age of nineteen Denis, who had been studying technique in the Julian School for two years, was engaged in writing philosophical articles on art which he published under the "nom de plume" of Pierre Louis. For twenty years he has continued these illuminating studies of modern art in its making, meanwhile producing his masterly mural decorations, easel pictures and illustrations. The fecundity of his creative power is only equaled by his seemingly unlimited capacity for production.

But his time at the first would be of limited duration: Denis found the teaching there much

◄ **Maurice Denis**,
The Muses, 1893.
Oil on canvas, 171.5 x 137.5 cm.
Musée d'Orsay, Paris.

too academic and left shortly afterwards. Meeting Paul Sérusier (1864 – 1927) at the "Académie Julian", Denis established around himself the Nabis group, which included among its members Pierre Bonnard (1867 – 1947), Edouard Vuillard (1868 – 1940), and Henri-Gabriel Ibels (1867 – 1936). Taking their name from the Hebrew word *nabi*, meaning "prophet", the Nabis sought spiritual paths in relation to modern doctrines and philosophies, particularly in relation to the East, Orphism, and esotericism. The group was also greatly influenced by the painting of Paul Gauguin. Sérusier, who would meet the master of Pont-Aven on a trip to Brittany, during the course of which he painted *Talisman* under Gauguin's sensible advice, shared what he learned then with the group.

In 1890, Maurice Denis reflected on the materiality and immaterialness of color, space and technology: *'A painting is essentially a tarpaulin surface covered by colors in a certain order.* In the same year, Denis exhibited for the first time at the *Salon des Artistes Français* and the same year he published the *Manifeste du Mouvement Nabi (Manifesto of the Nabi Movement)* in an issue of the journal *Art et Critique*, setting out his now famous definition: *"Remember that a painting, before it is a cavalry horse, a female nude, or any other subject, is primarily a flat surface covered with colours arranged in a certain order".*

The next year he exhibited in the "Salon des indépendants", followed by the Salon of *Les Vingt* in 1892. In accordance with his ideas, his works henceforth became highly decorative. He made several panels or cartoons for stained glass windows, in particular for Siegfried Bings' Art Nouveau gallery and at the request of Louis Comfort Tiffany. In 1893 he painted his *Muses* for Arthur Fontaine.

Always coloured by a deep spiritualism, in essence symbolic, the works of Denis, with their fragile lyricism, draw us into a world that has an atmosphere of unreality. With their simplified forms, marked halos, and colour harmonies, the works can make time stand still for those who look. In 1899 Denis started working on the decorations at Vésinet, first for the chapel of the college of Sainte-Croix, then for the church of Sainte Marguerite, while the year 1901 was marked by the *Homage to Cézanne (Hommage à Cézanne)* that he exhibited in the Salon of the "Société nationale des Beaux-Arts".

After the turn of the century, Denis made several tours, mainly in France, and still continued to produce a significant number of decorations, monumental compositions for townhouses, theatres and religious structures. Beginning in the 1920s he gave himself much more over to religious art.

Maurice Denis died in 1943 at the Cochin Hospital as a result of injuries sustained by being struck by a car. He left future generations a respected Œuvre that was highly personal and haunted by the religious interests that inspired him throughout his life. Not a very long life, counting by years, but Maurice Denis was the child of his age and his mental development, his grasp of modern problems has been of hot-house growth. It is a long call from these serious decorations to the theoretical tentatives of the undisciplined youth who threw himself with such fervor into the ranks of the Symbolists and fought so valiantly against worn-out academic dogmas. If it is true that this little coterie perpetrated many atrocities in the name of progress it is no less a fact that the much-abused Symbolists infused a new breath of life into the art of the nineties.

Maurice Denis, ▶
Portrait of Marthe Denis, the Artist's Wife or Suzanne with Yellow Houses, 1893.
Oil on canvas, 45 x 54 cm.
The Pushkin Museum of Fine Arts, Moscow.

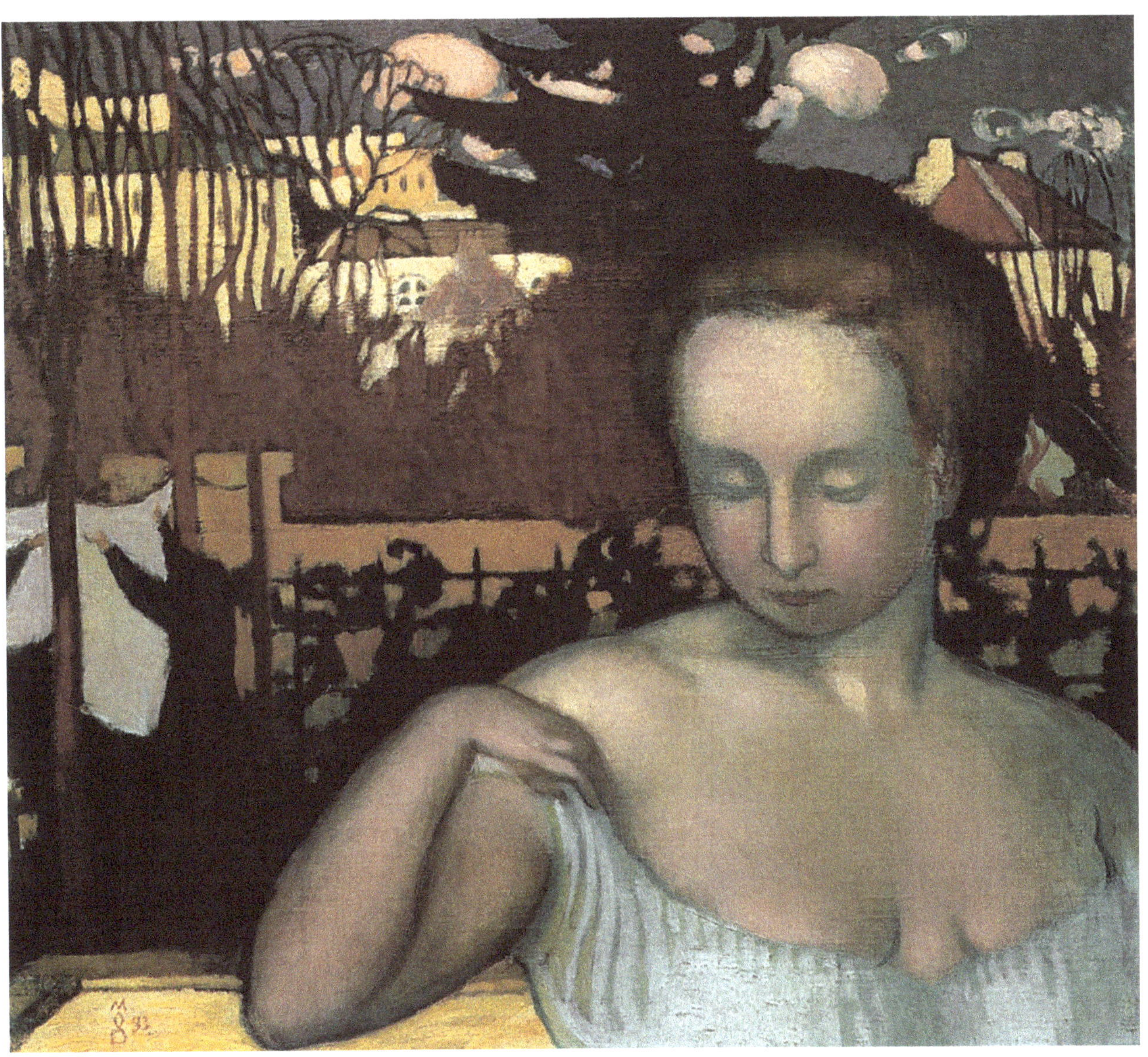

LIST OF ILLUSTRATIONS

A **Alexander, John White**

Isabel and the Pot of Basil, 1897.   14

B **Böcklin, Arnold**

Island of the Dead, 1880.   26

The Sacred Wood, 1882.   24

Seaside Villa, 1878   27

Burne-Jones, Edward

The Baleful Head, 1885-1887.   36

The Wedding of Psyche, 1895.   38-39

The Wheel of Fortune, 1883.   17

C **Carrière, Eugène**

Mass Theatre, 1895.   46

Meditation II. Portrait of a Girl.   44

The Motherly Kiss, 1898.   47

D **Denis, Maurice**

The Muses, 1893.   64

*Portrait of Marthe Denis, the Artist's Wife or Suzanne
with Yellow Houses,* 1893.   67

G **Gabriel Rossetti, Dante**

The Bower Meadow, 1850-1872.   35

Dantis Amor, 1860   32

Dante's Vision of Rachel and Leah, 1855   34

H   Hawkins, Louis Welden

The Halos, 1894.   9

K   Khnopff, Fernand

A Deserted Town, 1904.   51

I Lock My Door Upon Myself, 1891.   52-53

Study of Women, c. 1887.   50

M   Malczewski, Jacek

Thanatos I, 1898.   18

Moreau, Gustave

Galatea, 1880.   30

Œdipus and the Sphinx, 1864.   31

The Apparition, 1876-1898.   28

Munch, Edvard

Madonna, 1895-1902.   56

The Scream, 1893.   59

The Voice, 1893.   58

P   Pruszkowski, Witold

Falling Star, 1884.   4

Puvis de Chavannes, Pierre

St Genevieve Child in Prayer, 1877.   20

Young Girls at the Seaside, 1879.   23

R   **Redon, Odilon**

Closed Eyes, 1890.   43

Paul Gauguin, 1903-1905.   42

The Cyclops, c. 1898-1900.   40

S   **Schwabe, Carlos**

Sadness, 1893.   13

Spilliaert, Léon

The Crossing, 1913.   6

von Stuck, Franz

The Sin, 1893.   60

T   **Toorop, Jan**

Desire and Satisfaction, 1893.   54

V   **Vrubel, Mikhail Aleksandrovich**

Quick-Tempered Demon, 1901.   48

W   **Willumsen, Jens Ferdinand**

Fear of Nature. After the Storm, No. 2., 1916.   62

Sun in the Park, 1904.   10

ART HISTORY COLLECTION

Abstract Art

Art Deco

Art Nouveau

Baroque

Byzantine Art

Chinese Art

Cubism

Dada

Early Italian Art

Egypt Art

Expressionism

Gothic Art

Greek Art

Impressionism

Indian Art

Naive Art

Neoclassicism

Persian Art

Post-Impressionism

Realism

Renaissance

Pre-Raphaelites

Rococo

Roman Art

Romanesque Art

Romanticism

Surrealism

Symbolism

The Fauves

The Viennese Secession